To Pam –

May you enjoy many happy times in the kitchen! Remember our visit to Mendocino – a nice memory!

Love,
Antoinette

MORNING FOOD

from Cafe Beaujolais

Margaret S. Fox
and John Bear

Ten Speed Press

To Anne and Harold, for encouragement (with a little anxiety);
to Emily Fox, my favorite sister whom I admire so much;
and to Christopher Kump, my partner in chaos

1⊘

TEN SPEED PRESS
Post Office Box 7123
Berkeley, California 94707

Distributed in Australia by Simon & Schuster Australia; in Canada by Publishers Group West;
in New Zealand by Tandem Press; in South Africa by Real Books; in Southeast Asia by Berkeley
Books; and in the United Kingdom and Europe by Airlift Books.

Library of Congress Cataloging-in-Publication Data
Fox, Margaret S.
    Morning food / by Margaret Fox & John Bear.
        p. cm.
    ISBN 0-89815-309-3 — ISBN 0-89815-308-5 (pbk.)
    1. Breakfast. 2. Cafe Beaujolais (Mendocino, Calif.) I. Bear,
John, 1938- . II. Title.
TX733.F68 1990
    641.512 — dc20   89-36515
                                                       CIP

Book design and production by Fifth Street Design, Berkeley CA
The recipe and notes for China Moon Shanghai Rice on page 159 are copyright © 1989 by Barbara
Tropp

Photography at Cafe Beaujolais and around Mendocino copyright © 1990 by Brenton Beck and
J. Clifton Meek. Photograph of Cafe Beaujolais staff by Sean Sprague.
Printed in the United States of America
    5 6 7 8 9 10 — 98 97

CONTENTS

LIST OF RECIPES

ACKNOWLEDGMENTS

The passage of time brings with it change of great proportion. Change is necessary for growth, to be sure, but stability calms and remains a welcome state. The following people contributed to this stability and are very special in my personal and professional life. I owe thanks to:

My parents, Anne and Harold Fox, who never yelled at me once, even after I had moved into their kitchen to test eighty recipes and make a mess, for the kind of support and love only parents can provide;

My husband, Christopher Kump, who assured me that I would complete this book even when I wailed my doubts in the kitchen, who bailed me out of many a difficult situation, and who loves me in spite of my less-than-adorable qualities;

Patricia Priano, the restaurant's spirited left-handed manager and wine buyer, whose endurance in coping with typical daily crises, with long-term projects, and with *me* may result in sainthood (Tricia, I couldn't do it without you!);

Lorraine Ardaiz, the dedicated manager of Cafe Beaujolais Bakery, for her friendship, hard work, patience, loyalty and fun-to-be-withness;

My sister, Emily, who is simply *the best sister in the world*;

Stephanie Kroninger, a talented and creative graphic artist whose sense of whimsy and design are inspired;

Jose Manuel Yanez, patient and steady, whose generosity with his space in the kitchen allowed me to test these recipes;

The restaurant staff (my second family)—who are competent, caring, and upbeat overachievers;

Jocelyn Kamstra, Meadow Makovkin, and Roberta Wright, who as recipe testers only winced a few times when I asked them to ". . . do it again, but this time with a little less . . .";

Gina Salamone, without a doubt the world's most able bookkeeper and neophyte computer brain;

Everyone who donated special recipes for the world to appreciate;

Jaen Treesinger, the gardener at Cafe Beaujolais, whose vision has made plants, hummingbirds, people, and me happy for several years;

Neil O'Brien, also known as "Monsieur Bon Vivant" and "Big Hair," for his silliness and wisdom;

Sally-Jean Shepard, a great friend with a devilish sense of humor and complete professionalism;

Michael Potts, a computer wizard whose concern for the Bakery's progress and affection for the business have gently catapulted us into modern times;

Earl Thollander, the talented artist, whose magical drawings of Cafe Beaujolais and a stubborn gingersnap capture the essence of the restaurant's idiosyncratic personality;

Rick Steele for his towering clarity;

Mary Ellen Black, a special friend, for having the guts to follow her heart, even though it meant leaving a place she loved;

Our two and a half Black Labradors, Sanxi, Nini, and Willi, for their constant affection and willingness to try all cooking experiments;

Hilde, David, and Stephen Burton, dear friends for many years, for their appreciation and sensitivity;

Joana Bryar-Matons, big-hearted, and a wonderful cook too;

Eric and Friedel Goodman, for their enthusiasm for all my projects and their friendship over the years;

Barbara Tropp, who can make even a breakfast of toast and tea seem the most delicious meal ever;

Barbara Birchard, practitioner of acupressure who brings me back to earth every few weeks;

Morris Boynoff, whose sensibility and intelligence appeal to me a lot;

Charles and Catharine Martin, whose organically grown produce contributes enormously to the restaurant's quality;

Old Gold, store and staff, an oasis of beauty that graciously welcomes me even with cinnamon-encrusted fingernails;

KJAZ, the Bay Area's great jazz radio station, which kept me company for hours of recipe testing;

Stuart McKenna Nelson, who would have been so proud to see me now and who left so many memories;

Sam Shook, who I remember as a wonderful, gentle, strong person;

and especially the idea of Ocean Sanctuary as a permanent protection for the ocean, without which Mendocino would be just another spot on the map.

Food-stained recipe cards would have never made it from the kitchen of Cafe Beaujolais to the printed page had it not been for the enthusiasm, patience and inspiration of John Bear, one of the most fascinating people I know.

The staff at Cafe Beaujolais

INTRODUCTION

Take flour, butter, eggs, tomatoes, cheese, herbs, spices and a few other things, and you can make a nice traditional breakfast of a Spanish omelette and biscuits. Or you can make a lovely gooey slab of cold pizza. Take milk or cream, sugar, and chocolate and you can make a cup of steaming hot chocolate. Or you can make a bowl of ice cream with chocolate sauce.

At Cafe Beaujolais, my small but well-known restaurant in Mendocino, California (a tiny village 160 miles north of San Francisco, on the ocean), customers and national restaurant reviewers alike have for years been trying to figure out what makes the breakfasts so very special. Part of the answer is that at Cafe Beaujolais, we *don't* serve breakfasts, we serve *Morning Food.* We take ingredients that people have come to associate with the comfort and traditions of breakfast and mold and shape those ingredients into dozens of wonderful specialities whose only common thread is that they are utterly delicious—and they are served to our customers in the morning. The Morning Food philosophy gives people *permission* to eat a wide array of splendid things before the sun is high in the sky, without having to feel guilty about it.

Thousands of restaurants serve "breakfast all day." But how many serve "lunch all day" or "dinner all day"? Lunch and dinner dishes are rarely available at breakfast time. We have been trained that, if you want meat in the morning, it has to be called "breakfast sausage" or "breakfast steak" or "the Lumberjack Special." Ice cream or a *burrito* in the morning are clearly wrong and thus guilt-inducing.

The Morning Food philosophy says that you don't have to rationalize *any*thing you choose to put in your mouth before noon—but if you wish to justify this behavior, all you need to do is point out that you are eating exactly the same ingredients that other people *always* eat for breakfast; they have simply been put together in a different way. You can have your corn flakes and toast. Morning Food takes the corn and the bread, adds a few spices, and creates Tex-Mex Cornbread Pudding. You can have your bowl of stewed fruit and a cup of coffee with cream and sugar. Morning Food takes the apricots, the cream, and the sugar, throws out the coffee, and creates a Creamy Apricot Dessert Float.

Of course there is more to the success of Cafe Beaujolais than just Morning Food ... and there is more to Morning Food than just rearranging ingredients in interesting and unusual ways. Indeed, a lot of Morning Food *is* traditional breakfast fare: omelettes and muffins, waffles and *crêpes.* But there is a certain level of care and comfort in the restaurant—and in its recipes—that people find extremely satisfying and nurturing. Perhaps it takes them back to the mornings of their childhood, when life was simple and the day was new and Mom was there to see that everything was going to be all right. And if you *really* wanted last night's spaghetti cold for breakfast, you might get a hard stare, but then you'd also get an indulgent smile, and not feel guilty about declaring the spaghetti to be Morning Food after all.

This book runs the gamut from absolutely simple cinnamon rolls and chocolate coffee cake to elegant ice cream, fruit, and nut waffles; a complex pasta with goat cheese sauce; and an unexpected breakfast *burrito.* There are recipes for things that happen to be called soups, salads, sandwiches, and desserts—but they are all Morning Food, because it makes sense to serve them in the morning, and they *have* been served in the morning to legions of very happy eaters at the Cafe Beaujolais.

DISCLAIMER

Although some of the recipes in this book are quite simple to make, this is not necessarily a beginner's cookbook. I make this disclaimer in order to avoid feeling as if I have to explain every elementary thing about cooking.

For example, I assume that you already know how to fold egg whites into a batter. Many basic books are available these days, and no kitchen should be without one of them for reference.

Always be sure to read a recipe all the way through. Then make sure that all the ingredients are measured out and the utensils are at hand before you begin putting everything together. Nothing flummoxes a cook more than the discovery, just as the batter is ready and perceptibly deflating, that a special mold is crucial to the outcome.

IMPORTANT AND USEFUL ITEMS TO HAVE AROUND THE KITCHEN

People often seem interested in what equipment we have (and don't have) in the restaurant kitchen. Here's a basic list, with a few comments here and there.

WE HAVE:

- ❑ a sturdy wooden spoon, about fourteen inches long
- ❑ two wire whisks, one large, one small
- ❑ a flat-edged wooden spatula (great for nonstick pans)
- ❑ a large rubber spatula, about fourteen inches long
- ❑ a metal dough-scraper, used to clean off flat surfaces, to divide dough, and to chop
- ❑ aprons and, if you tend to be messy, a protective top (we all wear chef's coats and sometimes I think it would be better to wear a flameproof plastic outfit that could be hosed off at the end of the day)
- ❑ measuring cups and spoons
- ❑ small, medium, and large bowls
- ❑ sharp knives (paring, boning, chef's), a device to keep them sharp, and a willingness to use that device regularly
- ❑ a sieve, about 6- to 8-inches in diameter
- ❑ three thermometers: one for the oven, one for deep-fat frying and candy making, and an instant-read thermometer
- ❑ pots and pans with tight-fitting lids
- ❑ a scale
- ❑ a dependable timer (we use one that can time three different things at once)
- ❑ cutting boards (hint: if you place a wet dish towel underneath the board, it won't slide)
- ❑ a heavy-duty electric mixer
- ❑ a food processor (when I heard that Cuisinarts Inc. went bankrupt, I wondered if I should rush out and buy a dozen to get me through the next half century)

WE DON'T HAVE:

- ❑ a microwave oven.

This deficiency puts us in the minority these days. Some of our customers don't realize that we have no such high-tech creation in our little kitchen. Good food takes time to prepare. "Throw it in the microwave!" is not a phrase you will hear in our kitchen. You needn't check your pacemaker at the door.

MAIL-ORDER INFORMATION

We're talking about two kinds of mail-order products here: those splendid confections that we make ourselves in the Cafe Beaujolais Bakery, and those items made by our friends, neighbors, and suppliers, that we also sell by mail.

As tempting as it was to give detailed ordering information right here in the book, I chose not to for two good reasons: prices change, and items change, too. For instance, our own product line is expanding all the time and we add new suppliers from time to time, either to supplement or replace those we use now. So what makes the most sense is to ask you to write (or call) for our current mail-order catalogue. We will send it to you promptly, with order forms and complete instructions.

So, for complete information, please write or call:

Cafe Beaujolais Bakery
P.O. Box 730-M
Mendocino, California 95460
(707) 937-5614

Among the products available by mail are these:

Our own:
Panforte di Mendocino: an Italian nut confection in 22-ounce wheels, of almonds, walnuts, hazelnuts, or macadamia nuts.
Original Dried Fruit Fruitcake: a 24-ounce cake.
Chocolate Dried Fruit Fruitcake: also a 24-ounce wonder.

Our friends:
Grand Finale Buttercream Caramels: very special candy, available in various flavors, including mocha, chocolate, and bourbon pecan.
Fuller's Fine Herbs: artful blends of locally grown herbs. The one called Beaujolais Blend is mentioned frequently throughout this book and used regularly at Cafe Beaujolais.

CEREALS

MARGARET'S MÜSLI

Serves 1

This healthy cereal that originated in Europe and is sometimes spelled *muesli*, has been around for a great many years. The versions I've seen in the stores, even health food stores, have lots of sugar in them. I didn't think that was essential. This sugarless one is a tasty alternative. The only problem is that, as much as I like it, I sometimes feel as if I should be standing in a stable stall with the feed bag around my muzzle. If it isn't sweet enough, drizzle a teaspoon or so of maple syrup on the top before serving.

Most of the time, I serve this *müsli* with milk, but when stirred into yogurt, it makes quite a filling meal. Some people prefer to soak the oats in milk overnight, then add the rest of the ingredients in the morning, but that's altogether too mushy for me.

⅓ cup toasted oats (see below)	1 Tbsp. toasted nuts (try hazelnuts, walnuts, or almonds)
1 Tbsp. toasted wheat germ	
1 Tbsp. oat bran	
2 Tbsp. dried fruit (I like raisins and apricots)	1 tsp. maple syrup (optional)
	Milk or yogurt

Mix together everything but the maple syrup. Top with milk or stir into yogurt, then drizzle with maple syrup if you wish.

To toast oats: Place 3 cups rolled oats in a very thin layer in a 10- by 15-inch jelly-roll pan and bake at 350° for 15 to 20 minutes, or until lightly toasted. Stir the oats around once or twice while they are baking. These will keep in a tightly stoppered container.

BIRCHARD SOAKED OATS

Serves 1

John and Barbara Birchard live in Mendocino. Barbara is a respected acupressurist whom I've seen for a number of years; John is a noted door and window maker who recently completed his second book on, not unexpectedly, door making.

No one can eat fancy, rich food all the time. I have observed that, when people come into the restaurant four or five or six days in a row, they will after a while switch to lighter food such as waffles with fruit, or granola, or these simple and wholesome oats soaked in apple juice. Perhaps it cleanses the palate for another round of high living.

⅓ cup rolled oats (uncooked)
¼ cup apple juice
2 generous Tbsp. yogurt (unflavored or your choice of flavor)
1 drop vanilla extract

1 Tbsp. oat bran
1 heaping Tbsp. toasted almonds
1 heaping Tbsp. raisins or other dried fruit
Fresh fruit as desired: bananas, berries, or peaches

Soak the oats in the apple juice for 15 minutes, then add the rest of ingredients.

EMILY'S NORTHEASTERN BREAKFAST TREAT

Makes 1 serving

When my younger sister Emily and I were little, we read a story about an unhappy girl who was sent to live with her strict grandparents in New England. One of her few pleasures was pouring hot, freshly boiled maple syrup onto the snow, then eating it as sticky candy. To a Californian born and raised, who has not traveled much, tales of maple syrup actually coming from sap in trees seems romantic indeed, but I have become convinced it really happens that way.

My sister now lives all too far away, on the East Coast, where she has actually participated in the following exotic-sounding event. I realize most readers will not be able to do this because of geographical limitations, but now you have something splendid to look forward to one day, as do I.

1 maple tree	Butter
Bowl of hot cereal	Milk

Emily writes: "In the late winter when the sap is running, prevail upon a friend who is tapping trees to give you a quart of fresh sap. In addition to being a refreshing beverage, it can be used as the liquid in your favorite hot cereal recipe. The resulting flavor, a rich blend of nutty grain and subtle sweetness, is extremely satisfying and requires nothing more than a little butter or milk. This is what Maypo would like to be when it grows up."

KEEPING FOOD HOT

This is essential. Many Morning Food dishes really must be served piping hot or they suffer terribly. That's just as true at home as it is in the restaurant. In the restaurant, we don't use heat lamps or infrared gadgets, or anything like that. It's really *real* in our kitchen—just slightly more technical and on a somewhat larger scale than the home kitchen.

We don't use heating devices, because they don't help the quality of food. For instance, eggs tend to get rubbery under a heat lamp because you're continuing to heat the protein.

We keep the plates hot on a ledge that is part of our stove. They are hot all the time. At home, I would heat the plates in the oven (300° about 5 minutes) before using them. Some people run them under hot water for a while, or even use the drying cycle of the dishwasher.

Heating devices make one lazy. I have observed this in other restaurants; not my own. The waiting staff might think, "I don't have to rush, because it will stay hot." At Cafe Beaujolais, I want everything to go out *right this second*. Many is the time my dulcet tones can be heard shrieking, "This is *ready*. Will *no one* pick it up?"

FRUIT

CARAMELIZED APPLESAUCE

Makes 4 to 5 cups

APPLES

A lot of people grow apples in and around Mendocino. We have a couple of dozen apple trees on our property at home, including some varieties I had never heard of before, such as Winter Banana and Rhode Island Greening. Varieties that, for one reason or another, never made it into the commercial marketplace, although we are using them in the apple butter that we sell by mail.

Among the more readily available varieties, I like the Granny Smith because the apples don't turn to mushy slushy applesauce when you cook them.

Once I had the pleasure of working with Gaston LeNôtre, perhaps France's premier pastry chef, at the Great Chefs of France Cooking School, held at the Robert Mondavi winery. Everything he did had a touch of magic about it. My chunky applesauce is inspired by his. It is delicious as a topping for blintzes or *crêpes* or rice pudding, or stirred into yogurt or cottage cheese.

About 4 ½ lb. cooking apples
  (I use Granny Smith)
1 ⅓ cups water
Juice from half a lemon

2 cups sugar
½ vanilla bean, split in half
  lengthwise

Peel and core the apples and place peels and cores in a saucepan. Add water, bring to a boil, lower the heat, and simmer for 5 minutes. Cut each apple into 6 wedges, place in a bowl and toss with lemon juice, trying to coat each surface of every wedge.

Strain the cooking liquid from the peels and cores through a sieve over a large pan, pressing hard to extract as much liquid as possible. Add sugar to the liquid in the pan and bring slowly to a boil, stirring gently with a wooden spoon until the sugar melts. If any sugar sticks to the sides of the pan, clean it off with a moistened pastry brush.

When the syrup comes to a boil, raise the heat and boil rapidly for about 10 minutes until it reaches 313°, stirring occasionally. As soon as the syrup begins to turn a caramel color, add the apples and the vanilla bean. *Be very careful not to get any of this syrup on you. It is incredibly hot.* If you do, immerse the burned area in cold water immediately.

Cook for 5 minutes, then lower the heat and cook at a slow boil for about 20 minutes, or until the apples begin to fall apart. The finished sauce should be chunky, not smooth. Don't stir the apples; instead, shake the pan gently.

FIVE-SPICE APPLESAUCE

Serves 6 to 8

A PROLIFERATION
OF VARIETIES

We are always looking for ways to do something slightly different with our abundant local apple crop. I find good old-fashioned applesauce very satisfying, either all by itself or with plain yogurt. This particular version is very nice with Birchard Soaked Oats (page 20) or Margaret's Müsli (page 19), or served warm with a scoop of vanilla ice cream. (Yes, it is legal to eat ice cream in the morning, especially in dishes like this.)

The recipe comes to me from Kate O'Shea (a former classmate and close friend from my days at the University of California, Santa Cruz, who is currently the Special Projects Coordinator for the Christic Institute office in San Francisco) and Michael Gabel, her husband. They don't cook very much (they insist that one can have interests other than food!), but the things they do make are very special.

A PROLIFERATION OF VARIETIES

One of the real pleasures of cooking nowadays is that there are more and more varieties of things available: more kinds of apples; six colors of bell peppers; yellow and white tomatoes; seventeen kinds of lettuces. For much of this, we must thank a woman named Frieda Caplan who introduced the kiwi (then known as a Chinese gooseberry) to America and all manner of other new-to-us fruits and vegetables from around the world. Most new things come first to California and then spread around the country. A spy reports that, about a year ago, the first *radicchio* appeared in his supermarket in central Tennessee. Can grits with arugula be far behind?

8 apples (Pippins are a good choice)	½ tsp. allspice
1¾ cups apple juice	½ tsp. cloves
1 Tbsp. minced fresh ginger	½ tsp. crushed anise seeds
1½ tsp. cinnamon	Lemon juice to taste

Peel, seed, and core the apples and cut them into small chunks. Place all the ingredients, except the lemon juice, into a large saucepan fitted with a tight lid. Turn the heat to medium, cover the pan, and cook the apples until tender.

Mash with a potato masher or a wire whisk. Leave as chunky as desired. Season with lemon juice as you wish.

FRIED BANANAS

Serves 1 or, conceivably, 2

This recipe comes straight from the headquarters of Lily-Gilders, Inc. (My mother and I are officers of this organization whose mission is to make every food, no matter how good, just a little bit better.) You start with one basic banana and, by the time you are done, you have something that looks spectacular and tastes divine. There is no limit to the amount of gilding you are hereby given permission to do, on this particular banana-lily. The only caution is to move quickly while you are making it.

Eat this as is, on ice cream, or as a wonderful topping for pancakes and waffles.

1 medium banana, green-tipped
1 Tbsp. butter
2 to 3 tsp. lemon or lime juice
1 Tbsp. brown sugar, maple syrup, or honey
2 Tbsp. dark rum or brandy

Optional lily-gilding extras: cinnamon, nutmeg, toasted walnuts, sesame seeds, coconut, yogurt, sour cream, and/or ice cream

Peel the banana and cut it lengthwise, then crosswise, making 4 pieces. Melt the butter in small frying pan and brown the banana pieces quickly on both sides, about 2 minutes at most. Mix together the juice and sweetening and pour over bananas. Turn the bananas to coat both sides as the syrup bubbles and thickens. Heat the rum or brandy, pour it over bananas, and set it all on fire. Serve with a wide spatula. Pour the possibly-still-flaming sauce over. Garnish with any or all of the optional ingredients.

PAST-ITS-PRIME POACHED FRUIT À LA MOM

Serves 4 to 6

At one time or another, everybody has bought some fruit that looked wonderful in the store, only to get home, take a bite of it, and say, "Blecchhh." Once, when this happened to my frugal mom, she devised this recipe, which is a clever way of making something end up much better than one might have expected. Even though she is normally a very recipe-oriented person, this preparation can be quite spontaneous, so I hovered at her elbow, paper and pen in hand, as she tossed "a little of this" and "a little of that" into the pan.

Of course the recipe will work perfectly well with tasty in-season fruit, but it is hardly necessary. You could use cotton balls and it would probably turn out tasting really good. If you use more than one type of fruit, you may wish to retitle the recipe Poached Fruit Mélange. Use only fruit that has stones or pits or seeds: apples, peaches, pears, apricots, plums. It doesn't work with soft fruit such as strawberries or bananas, or pineapples.

The perfumed light syrup created during the cooking demands fresh whole spices. All too frequently, fragile spices sit in cupboards for years as the flavor slowly disappears, and dishes end up tasteless.

You might experiment with other wines, as well. Gewürztraminer makes this equally good, but quite different. Mom has even used jug wine. However you do it, you'll almost certainly come out with something that is better than the sum of its parts.

1 cup vermouth or dry white wine	¼ tsp. anise seed
1 cup water	Juice of half a lemon, about 2 Tbsp.
½ cup white sugar	Past-its-prime fruit: 4 pears, cored and peeled if you wish, and cut into quarters or slices, or an equivalent quantity of peaches, apples, apricots, or plums
1 cinnamon stick, about 3 inches long	
6 whole cloves	
15 cardamom seeds (remove the seeds from the whitish pods)	
3 whole allspice berries	

Place all the ingredients except the fruit into a large pot and simmer, uncovered, for about 5 minutes. Slice the fruit any way you wish. (Twelve slices for each pear makes an attractive presentation.) Add fruit, bring to a boil, cover, and turn the heat down. Simmer for about 3 to 5 minutes, or until fruit is tender. Cooking time depends on the size of the fruit slices and the ripeness of fruit, so check the fruit with a sharp knife to see if it is tender. When done, remove from heat and let cool.

Refrigerate for at least 8 hours before eating. Sometimes my mom adds 1 cup of blueberries or other berries after the fruit is removed from the heat.

POACHED APPLES AND PEARS WITH CRÈME FRAÎCHE

Makes 4 to 6 servings

This is a fresh fruit compote that you can make pretty much all year round, or at least as long as pears are available. You can make it the day before, and refrigerate it overnight. It can be served as an appetizer at the beginning of a meal or as the fruit accompaniment to an egg dish or other items of morning food. Served over cottage cheese, it could be the base for the main part of the meal.

It isn't that sweet. I tend to feel that cutting back on sugar is more important to the diet than many other so-called healthy things people do. The natural sweetness of the fruit and the honey makes this dish sweet enough. It doesn't need to be quite this rich; in fact the *crème fraîche* can be replaced with drained yogurt if you wish.

The white wine is a nice addition, because it balances all the flavors and refreshes your palate. Food that is entirely sweet or entirely tart is boring. I eat two bites and suddenly I've had enough of that.

One of the main problems in buying pears, especially out of season, is that they are too hard. But that is nothing to worry about for this recipe: the pears are poached, which should render them pleasant and juicy.

3 apples	¼ tsp. nutmeg
3 pears (preferably ripe but not mushy)	Zest of 1 lemon and 1 orange, finely chopped
2¼ cups apple juice	½ cup Crème Fraîche (see page 131) or drained yogurt (see side bar)
1 cup dry white wine	
2 Tbsp. honey	
1 cinnamon stick	¼ tsp. powdered cinnamon

Peel and core the apples and cut each into about 10 slices. Peel and core the pears and cut each into about 8 pieces.

Put the apple juice, wine, honey, cinnamon stick, and nutmeg in a large pot and bring to a boil. Reduce the heat and simmer for 10 minutes. Add the apple slices and citrus zest and simmer for about 5 minutes, until the apples are almost tender. Add the pear slices and poach for 3 minutes.

Pour into a bowl, and cover, and refrigerate overnight. Serve with a dollop of *crème fraîche* or drained yogurt and a dusting of powdered cinnamon.

DRAINED YOGURT

Put the yogurt (you might start with, say, four cups) in a fine mesh sieve, so that it can drain into a bowl. Leave it overnight in the refrigerator. The stuff that dribbles out is whey, as in "curds and." Whey can be used in making bread, wherever liquid is called for. In the restaurant, we add whey to the water that we mix into bread dough. Whey is full of protein and should not be wasted (wheysted).

The yogurt is reduced by about half through the draining process. You're left with very thick yogurt, thus much richer than it was before, but it isn't fat the same way that sour cream is. You can use it as a topping on fruit, as is, instead of sour or whipped cream.

RHUBARB GLOP

Makes about 1 quart

Many people grow rhubarb in this area, and I happen to think it is one of America's great underrated fruits, or vegetables, or whatever it is. Poor rhubarb has led a tortured life: most people, if they do anything at all with it, stew it with half a ton of sugar. It deserves a better fate.

My mom did the definitive research to demonstrate that rhubarb does not require immense amounts of sugar. One summer, she made batch after batch of stewed rhubarb, each one with a little less sugar than the last. By the end, very little sugar was required. Of course it was tart, but in quite a pleasant way.

This particular glop isn't exactly light on sugar, but one doesn't use a whole lot of glop at one time. It appears, for instance, as a relish for the Smoked Turkey Sandwich (see page 120). And it becomes the base of the Strawberry-Rhubarb Pie (see page 184), which has no additional sugar at all. I wouldn't want to eat this all by itself, but I have eaten it as a stand-alone dish, stirred up with plain yogurt which mellows it nicely. It will last in the refrigerator for up to six weeks, and it freezes well.

3 lb. fresh rhubarb	3 Tbsp. grated fresh ginger
2¼ cups sugar	6 Tbsp. lemon juice

Cut off the rhubarb leaves and wash the stalks. Cut the rhubarb into ½-inch chunks. In a large bowl, mix with sugar and cover with plastic wrap. Place in the refrigerator overnight.

Stir the mixture well, scraping the bowl to mix in any undissolved sugar, then place into a colander and drain directly into a saucepan. Place the rhubarb back into the bowl and bring the syrup in the pan to a boil. When all the sugar is dissolved, pour the syrup back over the rhubarb, stir, and let sit 15 minutes.

Drain through a sieve. Measure 1 cup of the syrup and return to a pot large enough to hold all the rhubarb too. (Save the rest of the syrup to make Rhubarb Syrup, page 200.)

Add the rhubarb, ginger, and lemon juice, stir, and cook over medium heat, stirring frequently, until the rhubarb is soft but is not mush. Let cool and store refrigerated.

FURTHER THOUGHTS ON STARTING A RESTAURANT

In my first book, I feel I may have been somewhat disparaging about getting involved in the food business. A number of reviewers said things such as, "If you've ever harbored the fantasy of moving to the country and opening a little restaurant, read this book first." But more than a few people told me, "I read that book, and *I'm* going to open my own restaurant now." I say, "Perhaps you didn't read it well enough."

People get involved in the food business because they think it has the potential of making them a lot of money. For a few, it does; for most, it continues to be a very grueling business, not an easy way to make a buck. But the commmodity involved is food, which people identify with. No one gets emotionally involved with a grommets, at least not in the way you identify with a chocolate cake.

"Me in the food business?" they say. "Why not, I eat food three times a day. I'm an expert." But it isn't like that at all. It is a *business*, which only happens to be food. In that sense, it really is much more closely aligned with the grommet business.

I fear for those people who suddenly find themselves running a business, with all the complexities and headaches that entails. Of course the food has to be there, and be good . . . but, when you and your staff are going crazy because of a late delivery or a

SAUSAGE-STUFFED BAKED APPLES

Serves 4

Somebody was recounting a recipe for baked apples and said, "Of course you cover the apples up, because you know how ugly they are." I replied that baked apples aren't ugly, they're homely. The serving staff sometimes says, "Oh, what happened to these?" Nothing happened, darn it. This is the way they are *supposed* to be.

This recipe is both homely and a little unusual, because it is sweet and savory at the same time. It can be a meal in itself, at any time of the day, or it can accompany waffles, pancakes, eggs, or French toast. It has no sugar in it; the sweetness comes from the apple itself and the frozen apple juice concentrate.

The chicken-apple sausages from Gerhard's Napa Valley Sausage Company in Yountville, California, are extra special. We have served them for several years, and even the most die-hard sausage haters are won over by these light and sweet delicacies. I am such a fan (I average one sausage a day) that I wanted to share them with the rest of the world, so you can now buy them by mail from the Cafe Beaujolais Bakery (see page xv). Whatever sausage you end up with, make sure it is flavorful and made with as few preservatives as possible.

Notice that we're not just coring the apple; we are creating a much larger space inside to hold a generous quantity of filling.

major price increase, it really doesn't matter whether the commodity is tomatoes or door-knobs.

I'm not saying the food is unimportant. Ulti-mately, it is *the* most im-portant thing, in the sense that if it isn't right, people won't come back. But it is only one of many factors. A really glitzy new restaurant opened in Berkeley, recently. Not one penny was spared on the decor. It is truly a spectacular place of its kind, that virtually acts as a vacuum to suck people in off the street. And what happens when you are inside? Dreadful food, rather indifferently pre-sented and served. If the owners had taken a tenth of their chandelier budget to hire a good chef, their chances of sur-vival would have been dis-tinctly improved.

4 baking apples, similar in size (Rome Beauty or Golden Delicious)	¼ cup currants
1 Tbsp. butter	2 tsp. freshly and finely grated ginger
1 cup minced yellow onions	⅔ cup apple juice concentrate, straight from the can (do not dilute)
⅓ cup finely chopped celery	
4 oz. sausage	

Preheat the oven to 275°. Core the apples, leaving the bottom stem intact to allow the apple to hold the filling securely. Enlarge the hole with a small knife to create a space about 2 inches deep and 2 inches across. Make sure that the apple wall is at least ½ an inch thick. Peel the outside of each apple about halfway down. Chop up the apple "insides" and set aside.

There was really only one very negative letter, on the theme of "how dare you take credit for making Cafe Beaujolais a success, when it clearly was due entirely to the previous owners." It came from a young man who had worked at the restaurant before I took over. Otherwise, the only criticisms have been from people who think that the food is too abundant ("Remember the starving children of . . . ") or too rich ("Remember the high-cholesterol-count stockbrokers of . . . ") , or that I hate children ("Of course they are going to yell in the dining room. . . ").

People who take the time to write are either happy, or they have a specific question about a recipe, or want something clarified, such as the woman who was unclear about the difference between bitter chocolate and bittersweet chocolate (bittersweet is just a little sweeter).

I'm a letter writer myself, and partly because of the experience of being a letter-*receiver* from my readers, I find myself writing to authors whose books I've loved. The last one was to Rosalind Creasy. I was just transfixed by her book, *Food from the Garden,* in which she talks about growing things in your garden specifically for food preparation. She clearly put her heart and soul into this book, and it comes out on every single page. It gave me a million new cooking ideas.

Melt the butter over medium heat in a large skillet and add the onions. Sauté for about 5 minutes, then add the celery and apple insides and continue cooking for another 5 minutes until soft. Add the currants, ginger, and ¼ cup of the apple juice concentrate and bring to a boil. Cook over high heat for about 30 seconds, until the liquid thickens a bit. Set aside.

Sauté the sliced or crumbled sausage until browned and add to apple mixture. Stir to combine. Divide among the four apples and place them in an 8- by 8-inch pan. Mix the remaining concentrate with ½ cup water and pour in bottom of pan. Bake for about 1 to 1½ hours. Baste the apples generously with the liquid several times during the baking. If the tops start to brown, cover them with foil. Test apples with a knife. When it goes in easily (no crunch), they are done. Let sit at room temperature until warm, then serve, or let cool, then refrigerate. Cover the whole apple in foil and reheat to serve.

COOKIES & BISCUITS

BREAKFAST COOKIES *Makes about 5½ dozen*

Now you have permission to eat cookies for breakfast. All the ingredients are things that you might eat for breakfast anyway. In fact, I've been known to eat the Grapenuts plain, or with milk, before they ever got into the cookie dough. There are a lot of ingredients, because the idea is to make these a complete breakfast. If you had some citrus, some milk, and a handful of these, you'd be in pretty good shape providing you know when to stop reaching into the cookie jar. (Of course to get your basic two eggs, you'd have to eat eleven dozen cookies.)

These cookies are very crunchy, as you might expect from the Grapenuts. If that bothers you, you could easily substitute a cup of some crunchy flake cereal. I prefer currants to raisins; they seem to distribute the sweetness more evenly throughout the cookies.

½ cup butter	2½ cups white flour
⅔ cup brown sugar	1 tsp. baking soda
1 egg	1 tsp. salt
1 cup vegetable oil	⅓ cup + 1 Tbsp. toasted wheat germ
1 tsp. vanilla extract	
1 cup regular rolled oats, toasted (see page 19)	⅓ cup + 1 Tbsp. oat bran
1 cup Grape-Nuts cereal	⅓ cup + 1 Tbsp. nonfat dry milk powder
½ cup peanut butter (optional, but you'd be nuts to leave it out)	1 cup raisins or currants
	1 cup toasted, chopped walnuts

Preheat oven to 350°. Cream the butter and sugar. Add the egg, then the oil and vanilla. Stir in the remaining ingredients.

Form into balls between 1 to 3 inches in diameter. Place on ungreased cookie sheets and flatten with a fork. Bake for 12 to 18 minutes, depending on the size of the cookie. Check the bottoms. Because they are very brown to begin with, you must watch this closely. Remove from the pan and let cool.

LOCALS VERSUS TOURISTS

On weekdays, we get more locals than tourists for breakfast. They get up earlier, for one thing. Also, there are more and more bed and breakfast inns in the area. People are paying for their breakfast, they may as well eat it. However some innkeepers tell me it isn't uncommon for people to skip their prepaid one . . . or even to have, say, the inn's croissant, fruit and coffee early in the morning, and then head into town for yet another breakfast at the Cafe Beaujolais.

On the weekends, there are far more tourists, both because it is the logical time for travel, and because the locals seem to prefer to come here when it is less crowded.

ORANGE BISCUITS

Makes 12 biscuits

This recipe was originally called Spicy Currant Biscuits, but there was something not quite right with them. The solution turned out to be the omission of the currants entirely. This was a major improvement indeed, but necessitated a name change. Actually there should probably be another name adjustment, because these aren't exactly biscuits; they taste much richer than the average biscuit. More in the direction of a scone, you might say, although lacking the eggs of a traditional scone. Perhaps we have invented the *biscone*, which sounds slightly more appetizing than the *sconcuit*.

Please remember that the most important thing about biscuits is to handle the dough as little as possible. Combine the ingredients and knead the dough quickly and you'll be on your way to light, flaky whatever-they-ares.

1¾ cups unsifted white flour	¼ cup unsalted butter, cut into ½-teaspoon-sized pieces and frozen
3 Tbsp. white sugar	
¼ tsp. nutmeg	¾ cup + 1 Tbsp. heavy whipping cream
1 Tbsp. baking powder	
1 tsp. salt	1 Tbsp. freshly and finely grated orange rind

Preheat the oven to 325°. In the bowl of a food processor fitted with an S-blade, place the flour, 2 Tbsp. of the sugar, nutmeg, baking powder, and salt. Blend. Add the butter and process for a few seconds, until the mixture is the texture of coarse meal. Add ¾ cup of the heavy cream and the orange rind. Process just until dough forms.

Turn out onto a lightly floured board and knead about 5 times. Roll out to a thickness of ¾ inch, keeping the shape as square as possible (the biscuits will be more attractive). Cut into 12 pieces and place on an ungreased baking sheet. Brush with 1 Tbsp. heavy cream and sprinkle with 1 Tbsp. sugar. Bake for about 15 to 18 minutes, or until golden brown.

CORNMEAL BISCUITS
Makes about 16 biscuits

These are not your conventional biscuits. They have more texture than a buttermilk biscuit does. But they are made in just the same way as ordinary biscuits, which means they are fast and simple — the sort of thing you can do in the morning and serve them fresh and hot. You could even mix the dry ingredients the day before if you wish.

I've given up making round biscuits. Since you're not supposed to touch the dough that much, why labor over a shape that requires more handling than most, not to mention the fact that you end up with all those little bits and pieces and lopped off-corners? Furthermore, the second batch of biscuits, made from the scraps left over from cutting round ones, never seems to come out as good.

Cornmeal complements a lot of different flavors. I would serve these biscuits with cheese, or with eggs and salsa, or an omelette filled with my Black Bean Chili (page 158). The corn gives it some additional pizzazz. The little bit of sugar, incidentally, is there to brown the biscuits rather than to sweeten them. That's one of the chemical roles that sugar plays.

1¾ cups unsifted white flour
1 Tbsp. white sugar
¼ cup cornmeal
1 Tbsp. baking powder
¼ tsp. baking soda
1 tsp. salt

⅓ cup unsalted butter cut into ½-teaspoon-sized pieces and frozen
½ cup buttermilk
1 egg

Preheat the oven to 425°. In the bowl of a food processor fitted with an S-blade, place all the dry ingredients. Blend. Add butter and process for a few seconds, until mixture is the texture of coarse meal. Mix together the buttermilk and egg, and add. Process for a few seconds, just until dough forms. Turn out on a lightly floured board and knead about 5 times. Roll out to a thickness of ¾ inch, keeping the shape as square as possible (your biscuits will be more attractive). Cut into 16 pieces, place on an ungreased baking sheet, and bake for 15 to 18 minutes, until golden brown.

at the time, rather than by writing a letter two or three weeks later, when all I can say is that I'm sorry, and then I go around feeling bad. If someone in the restaurant says, "I just can't eat this, it has too much garlic," or, "This just isn't what I thought it would be," or, "The toast is too brown," then we will make it right. That's the goal of the restaurant; not to run a minor soap opera that tries to upset or infuriate the patrons.

I do point this out to people who write complaint letters and I can only hope that they will think about these things the next time they are unhappy in a restaurant. Curiously, no one has ever responded to my response letters.

MUFFINS

BRAN MUFFINS

Makes 1 dozen muffins

Perhaps the world is overwhelmed by bran muffins, or anything with oat bran, at this point. But this is a great little recipe. The coffee in the batter is unusual. When combined with the other ingredients, it doesn't taste like coffee, but does give the muffins a deeper flavor. Also, I confess, it lures me into eating a little bit of the batter before it turns into muffins.

I cut the sugar back in this recipe; my feeling is that many sweet things are just *too* sweet.

It is really important not to overbeat the batter; just stir until blended. Beaten batter results in ugly muffins, with funny-looking tops and big gaping holes inside. I get neurotic about this in the restaurant, because we use a big powerful mixer and, if someone is distracted or just turns away for a moment, there goes the batter and there is no way to repair it.

CLOSE, BUT NO C - BAR

There two schools of thought on muffin baking: those who spray nonstick stuff in the pan, and those who use papers. I prefer papers, but have no problem with those who don't.

In my first book, I offered a dozen Congo Bars to anyone who could provide me with a fool-proof way of keeping muffins from sticking to the pan. That offer produced a lot of letters, including more than a few terse directions: "Use Pam; now send me my Congo Bars."

1 egg	1¼ tsp. baking soda
⅓ cup brown sugar	3 Tbsp. oat bran
¼ cup vegetable oil	1½ cups bran cereal (such as
½ cup strong coffee	All-Bran)
1 cup buttermilk	½ cup raisins, dried prunes, or
½ tsp. salt	any other dried fruit
2¼ cups unsifted white flour	

Mix the egg, sugar, oil, coffee, buttermilk, and salt. Sift together the flour and baking soda, stir in the bran and bran cereal, and add this mixture to the liquid ingredients. Stir just until blended. Quickly stir in raisins. Let the batter sit refrigerated overnight. Scoop into prepared muffin tins and bake at 400° for about 20 minutes.

OATMEAL-RAISIN MUFFINS

Makes about 1 dozen muffins

This is probably the most widely distributed recipe I shall ever publish. It was prepared for the Pacific Gas and Electric Company's newsletter, which is mailed to untold millions of households along with the utility bill. If you're one of them, I apologize for being redundant, but it is a fine little recipe for a simple muffin. We make them all the time at Cafe Beaujolais.

I don't think you can ever have too many muffin recipes. These are especially nice when you're doing a more elaborate breakfast, because they are so fast and easy to make. The batter lasts well, so you could make it the night before.

I am pleased to see buttermilk available in pint-sized containers, because I am often asked the question, "But what do I do with the rest of the buttermilk? Do I have to make one of your chocolate cakes?" Things could be worse.

Incidentally, the effect of that PG&E mailing was quite extraordinary, in terms of letters, phone calls, and visits to the restaurant. Unlike the articles about us in publications such as *Gourmet* magazine, the gas bill hits everybody. It does not discriminate on the basis of food sophistication. And a lot of people came in who might never have done so otherwise.

1 cup rolled oats	½ tsp. cinnamon
1 cup buttermilk	2 eggs, beaten lightly
¾ cup white flour	⅓ cup light brown sugar
½ tsp. baking powder	6 Tbsp. melted butter
¼ tsp. salt	⅓ cup raisins
¾ tsp. baking soda	

Combine the oats and buttermilk and let stand 30 minutes.

Sift together the flour, baking powder, salt, baking soda, and cinnamon. Stir the eggs into the buttermilk mixture, then add sugar, the butter, and the flour mixture. Stir until just combined. The batter will be lumpy. Fold in the raisins.

Spoon into a muffin tin, filling the cups about two-thirds full. Bake at 400° for 15 to 20 minutes.

NAME THAT MUFFIN

Makes about 18 muffins

The personality of this muffin changes depending on the fruit or vegetable that is added to the batter. Currently, it is my favorite muffin for two reasons. One is because it tastes so great, the ginger being a key reason. And the other is that when we have leftovers we're dying to get rid of, or bruised but still edible fruits or vegetables, this is where they go. So far, we've used apples, pears, oranges, zucchini, tomatoes, plums, even fresh pumpkin. Keep experimenting.

One interesting option is to divide the batter into several batches and add different fruits or vegetables to each batch.

2 cups unsifted white flour
¾ tsp. salt
¾ tsp. baking soda
¼ tsp. baking powder
2 eggs
¾ cup brown sugar
¾ cup corn oil
¾ tsp. vanilla extract

1⅓ cups prepared fruit or vegetables
1½ tsp. cinnamon
1½ tsp. ground ginger
⅓ cup poppy seeds
¾ cup coarsely chopped toasted walnuts

Preheat oven to 400°.

Sift together the flour, salt, baking soda, and baking powder. In a separate bowl, whip the eggs with the sugar and oil. Stir in the vanilla, whatever fruits or vegetables you are using ,the spices, and the poppy seeds. Then add the flour mixture and the nuts. Do not overmix.

Spoon the batter into greased or papered muffin cups, filling each about three-quarters full. Bake for 25 to 30 minutes until golden brown.

VARIATIONS

Apple or pear: Core and shred them.

Zucchini: Shred them unpeeled.

Oranges: Wash well, chop up (skin, pulp, and juice), and process in the bowl of a food processor using steel S-blade. Add ⅓ cup extra poppy seeds, 1 extra tsp. ginger, and ½ extra tsp. cinnamon.

Pumpkin: Steam fresh pumpkin and cut into small bits.

Tomato: Cut them into small bits.

HOT-FROM-THE-OVEN MORNING MUFFINS

Makes about 15 muffins

The creator of this muffin recipe is a writer born and bred in New York, who, by her own admission, is temporarily marooned on the West Coast in San Francisco. (You could do worse.) Her publisher knows her as F. L. Florian, her *nom de plume* for murder mysteries. Under the name of Susan Sobel-Feldman, she writes short stories and book reviews and, on a more mundane level, has evolved a muffin repertoire for her husband's breakfasts. These sturdy muffins, filled with good flavors, will get you off to a steady start. They are delicious freshly baked, reheated, or toasted.

3/4 cup dried currants
1/3 cup orange juice
1/2 cup oat bran
1/2 cup raw wheat germ
1/2 cup cornmeal
1/2 cup whole wheat flour
1 cup white flour
1 Tbsp. baking powder
1/2 tsp. baking soda
1/2 tsp. salt

1 cup coarsely chopped, toasted pecans
1 egg, beaten
1/4 cup melted butter
1/4 cup light molasses
1 Tbsp. honey
1 1/2 cups buttermilk
2 Tbsp. finely grated orange peel (packed)

Preheat the oven to 375°.

In a small pan, gently simmer the currants in the orange juice for 5 minutes and set aside. Most of the juice will be absorbed.

Sift together the bran, wheat germ, cornmeal, flours, baking powder, the soda, and salt, then add the pecans.

In a separate bowl, combine the remaining ingredients and the currants and juice. Add the liquid ingredients to the dry and stir just enough to combine.

Spoon the batter into prepared muffin cups, filling them about three-quarters full; they don't rise much during baking. Bake for about 20 minutes.

APPLE BUTTER-RAISIN-NUT MUFFINS

Makes about 20 muffins

A couple of years ago, Chris and I were faced with a ton (this is not an exaggeration) of apples from our own orchard. We devised two ways to use them. One is an unusual apple butter using antique varieties such as Rhode Island Greening, King, Tompkins, Winter Banana, and Baldwin. This we sell through our mail order business (see page xv). The other is a series of recipes to use apple butter, such as this one, and Apple Butter Bread Pudding (see page 181).

It is really important to stir the ingredients just enough to smooth out the batter. In the restaurant's recipe file, this recipe is annotated, in big yellow letters:

Do not overmix or Margaret will have a nervous breakdown.

Bear that in mind, please.

Commercial apple butters vary considerably in sweetness, so you may wish to adjust the sugar in this recipe. Sometimes, when needing just a small quantity of apple juice, I will use one of those frozen concentrates and scoop out what I need, returning the rest to the freezer.

2 eggs	1 tsp. salt
¾ cup apple butter	¾ tsp. cinnamon
¾ cup apple juice	¾ tsp. nutmeg
⅓ cup corn oil	⅓ cup dry bread crumbs
½ cup white sugar	¼ cup oat bran
⅓ cup brown sugar	⅔ cup raisins or currants
2¼ cups white flour	1⅓ cups toasted walnuts
1 Tbsp. baking powder	chopped into pieces large
1 tsp. baking soda	enough still to be crunchy

Preheat the oven to 375°. Combine the eggs, apple butter, juice, oil, and sugars. Sift together the flour, baking powder, soda, salt, cinnamon, and nutmeg. Stir in crumbs and bran. Add dry ingredients to wet and stir just until smooth. Mix in raisins or currants and walnuts. Pour into a muffin tin that has been either sprayed with nonstick spray or lined with muffin papers and bake for 20 to 25 minutes, until a deep golden brown.

$12 FOR A BREAKFAST?!

We've helped combat the inevitable rise in Morning Food prices by introducing an "Early Bird Special" on weekdays: $3.25 (in 1989, anyway) for a nice basic breakfast.

Once in a while, I hear someone exclaiming over the size of the bill: "Twelve dollars for breakfast!" Wondering whether I am not, after all, gouging an unsuspecting public, I check the order: a double Caffe Fantasia, an almond croissant, the special omelette, and a gigantic fresh orange juice. Anyway, the prices are right there on the menu, so there shouldn't be any surprises.

STINSON BEACH BLUEBERRY MUFFINS

Makes about 2 dozen

When you get fresh ber-
ries and plan to use them
in batter, it really helps if
you freeze them first for
at least one and a half
hours. Then they don't
bleed all over your batter
as you stir them in. Even
when the berries them-
selves are an attractive
color, be prepared for the
batter to end up a less
than wonderful color
when you're done. For in-
stance, the blue of blue-
berries turns batter a
pallid gray when cooked.

These muffins, crunchy on top, are sublime, in large part due to the whipping cream. They came to me from my friend, Leslie Martin, a food and wine writer, who collected the blueberries one beautiful afternoon at Stinson Beach, on the coast north of San Francisco.

2 eggs	1 cup white flour
½ cup brown sugar	1 cup whole wheat flour
½ cup vegetable oil	1 Tbsp. baking powder
1 cup heavy whipping cream	1 cup chopped and toasted nuts
1½ tsp. vanilla extract	1 cup fresh blueberries that you
¼ tsp. ground nutmeg	have frozen

Preheat oven to 400°.

In a large bowl, mix together the eggs, sugar, oil, cream and vanilla. Set aside.

In another bowl, sift together the nutmeg, flours, and baking powder. Add the egg mixture to the flour bowl and stir quickly—just enough to blend ingredients—for about 15 to 20 seconds.

Fold in the nuts and frozen berries and pour into muffin tins prepared either with papers or nonstick spray. Bake for 18 to 20 minutes, until golden.

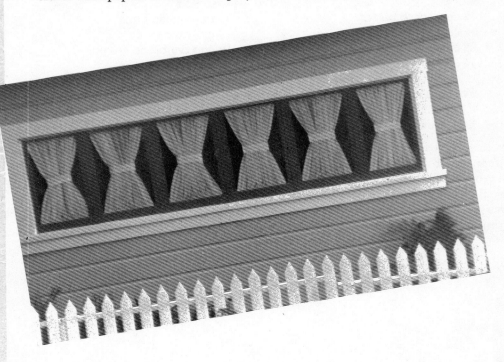

MOCHA WALNUT WONDER MUFFINS

Makes about 16 muffins

This may be the first and only cookbook to mention Robert Redford *and* Stevie Wonder. Anni Amberger has been cooking virtually her entire life and a few years ago she found herself cooking at a small café in Oakland frequented by musicians. One day, she heard that Stevie Wonder was coming in, so she invented these muffins in his honor. They were a grand success, and he took a bunch of them home.

My only alteration was to add more chocolate. If there is going to be any chocolate in a muffin, I really want to know it's there. The chocolate chips make it more of a cupcake than a muffin, but you can eat it at any time of the day.

3 eggs	1¼ cups whole wheat flour
¾ cup oil	1 cup brown sugar
1 cup buttermilk	½ tsp. baking powder
½ cup strong black liquid coffee	1 tsp. baking soda
1 tsp. vanilla extract	1 tsp. salt
⅓ cup cocoa (sifted, then measured)	1 cup chopped walnuts
1½ cups white flour	1 cup chocolate chips (optional)

Combine the eggs, oil, buttermilk, coffee, and vanilla and set aside.

Sift the rest of the ingredients, except for the nuts and chocolate chips, into a separate bowl. Add the nuts and chocolate chips. Add the dry mixture to the wet and mix quickly. Do not dawdle and do not overmix.

Spoon the batter into prepared muffin tins and bake at 375° for about 20 to 25 minutes or until done. Test with a toothpick inserted into the center of the muffin. When it comes out clean, the muffins are done.

WE'RE LOSING THE MORNING CHOCOLATE RACE

We Americans seem to restrict our early morning consumption of chocolate to hot chocolate. In other, clearly superior societies, the populace is less abstemious. In France, we were served chocolate sandwiches: buttered bread with chocolate sauce. And of course there is *pain au chocolat*: chocolate croissants for breakfast. In Holland, they sprinkle powdered chocolate rather generously over fruit and hot applesauce and serve it for breakfast. Get with it, America!

BREAD

BASIC SWEET-ROLL DOUGH

Makes 3¼ lb. of dough

Food memories are the strangest things. Have you ever, as an adult, tasted something that you loved as a child, to find that it just doesn't taste all that good? A disheartening experience occurred with the original recipe for sweet-roll dough—one that I fondly remembered from twenty years ago. How do I know it was twenty years ago? I was completely preoccupied making the dough, and my mother was shouting, "Margaret, Margaret, come and watch; a man is walking on the moon." However even that was not enough to make the original recipe merit inclusion in this book because the dough tasted heavy and dull.

Five versions later, I finally arrived at the following recipe, which was a good thing, because my father had begun to dread yet another unsuccessful cinnamon roll. This basic dough has thousands of possible uses, among them Cinnamon Rolls (see page 53), Cinnamon Raisin Bread (see page 54), and Almond- or Chocolate-filled Coffee Cake (see page 74).

2 Tbsp. dry yeast (check the expiration date to avoid grief)	¾ cup warm milk
½ cup sugar	½ cup instant nonfat dry milk powder
¼ cup warm water	2 tsp. salt
½ cup melted butter	4 eggs
1 Tbsp. grated orange peel (optional)	About 5½ cups white flour

In a small bowl, dissolve the yeast with a pinch of the sugar in warm water (about 110°). Stir and set in a warm place (about 80°) until foamy, about 5 minutes.

In a 4-quart bowl, using a wooden spoon, mix together the rest of the sugar, the butter, optional orange peel, warm milk, dry milk powder, salt, eggs, 3 cups of flour, and the yeast mixture. Add 1 cup of flour and beat like crazy (that is: *beat* not *stir*) for about 5 minutes, until dough strands come away from the sides of the bowl. This is an indication that the gluten, which is essential to the production of a springy dough with a fine crumb, is developing.

Gradually add up to 1½ more cups of flour. Various conditions, such as the weather and the absorbency of the flour, will determine the quantity of flour you'll need, so don't do anything rash such as dumping in all the flour at once. When the dough starts to pull away from the sides of the bowl, turn it out onto a lightly floured board and knead, adding a little flour if dough begins to stick. You must knead the dough for 5 minutes after your final addition of flour. The goal is a smooth, unsticky round of dough with air bubbles under the surface.

Place the dough in a greased bowl and cover with a damp towel or a piece of plastic wrap. Let it rise in a warm place until it has about doubled in size (about 1½ hours). Don't worry if the time is more or less; working with yeast is extremely imprecise. When risen, punch the dough down. If you are not ready to proceed, cover and let it rise again, for about an hour. (The second rising always takes less time and will produce a finer, more delicate crumb.) Punch the dough down, turn it out, and knead a few times to release air bubbles.

The dough is now ready to be made up into its final form. The following recipe, for Cinnamon Rolls, is an example.

CINNAMON ROLLS

Makes about 12 rolls

These are big, generous cinnamon rolls with a lot of stuff in them. If things like this don't have enough filling, somehow I feel cheated. To those people who think there is *too* much filling, I can only remind them forcefully that these are cinnamon rolls, not Ry-Krisp. And if you'd like even *more* filling . . . well, these can be just as decadent as you like.

I like this powdered sugar glaze, but then I'm not such a fan of goopy, gloppy stuff. This amount seems enough to make the finished product look and taste good. But if goopy gloppy is your style, then you can certainly make more of the glaze and ladle it on to your heart's content.

This recipe calls for half of the Basic Sweet-Roll Dough recipe (page 51). Of course you can double it, or you might want to make one pan of these and one loaf of Cinnamon Raisin Bread (page 54) or any other sweet dough recipe.

4 Tbsp. melted butter
1⅔ cups brown sugar
1½ Tbsp. cinnamon
Half of the Basic Sweet-Roll
   Dough recipe (page 51)
   (cover the other half with a
   towel until you are ready to
   use it)
1 cup raisins or currants
¾ cup walnuts

POWDERED SUGAR GLAZE
½ cup powdered sugar
   (measured, then sifted)
1 tsp. softened butter
⅛ tsp. vanilla or almond extract
About 1 Tbsp. hot water
¼ tsp. corn syrup

Preheat oven to 350°.

In a bowl, mix together the butter, sugar, and cinnamon.

Roll the dough out to a 12- by 15-inch rectangle. Sprinkle sugar and cinnamon mixture evenly over the surface of the dough, making sure to go all the way out to the edges. Sprinkle the raisins and walnuts over the sugar and pat everything lightly into the dough. Starting from the narrow side, tightly roll the dough. If anything edible falls to the counter, scoop it up and place it back on the dough.

Cut the roll into 12 slices and place in a greased 9- by 13-inch pan, cut-side up. Push any surface raisins into the dough, otherwise, they will burn and taste terrible. Cover the pan with a towel and let the rolls rise in a warm place until they are extremely light (about 1 hour).

Bake for about 35 minutes or until richly browned. If you are planning to serve the rolls at once, mix together with a spoon all the ingredients for the Powdered Sugar Glaze and drizzle it over them. Or dust them with powdered sugar. Serve warm.

SLICING BREAD

People ask me how I slice bread. Do they think I have some secret method that I might reveal just to them? Laser beams? Dental floss? Let the world know that I slice bread with a very sharp serrated knife, commonly and cleverly called a bread knife.

CINNAMON RAISIN BREAD

Makes 1 loaf

In the restaurant, after years and years of fussing around with fancy $400 industrial-strength toasters that were too delicate to be really reliable, we went to the discount store and bought a bunch of $12.59 Farberware home toasters. They are almost as reliable as the fancy ones. Of course Farberware doesn't send out a repairman to fix a $12 toaster . . . but then, come to think of it, neither did the manufacturers of the fancy one. "You live where?" they would say incredulously on the phone.

Because toast cools off so quickly, most restaurants (and indeed most homes) end up serving it cold. (A customer, Jim Campbell, was the first to identify those metal racks on which many European restaurants serve their toast as, actually, toast chillers.) So the toast station at the restaurant is one of the most complex stations we have. There are the cheap toasters. There is a warming tray. There is a pot of melted butter with a brush. There is a toaster oven. And there are little notes on scraps of paper that say things like "Dry" and "This is mine" and "Do not butter" and "Do not touch." When we're really busy, I admire but cannot imagine how the waiting staff handles it. Of course there are frequent plaintive cries of "Where's my toast?" and "Who buttered this toast?" and "Now I can't use this toast; does anyone else need it?" Once in a while we are enveloped in billowing

I may own a restaurant and have two cookbooks to my name, but that doesn't mean I have all the answers. For some reason, no matter how tightly I roll the dough for this bread, it tends to unfurl while it bakes. Sometimes it doesn't. I haven't figured out why. But I can say emphatically that it is just as good *unfurled* as it is furled. So if yours unfurls, tell your house guests that it took years to perfect this famous unfurled cinnamon raisin bread.

It is good toasted, but not in a conventional toaster, because the raisins keep wanting to fall out and get lost deep in the mechanism.

Half the Basic Sweet-Roll Dough recipe (page 51)	1 Tbsp. cinnamon
1 cup brown sugar	2 Tbsp. melted butter
	1 cup raisins

Preheat the oven to 350°. Lightly grease a 9- by 5-inch bread pan. Roll the dough out to a 12- by 15-inch rectangle. Mix the brown sugar, cinnamon, and melted butter. Sprinkle the sugar mixture evenly over the surface of the dough making sure to go all the way out to the edges. Sprinkle raisins over the sugar and pat everything lightly into the dough.

Starting from the narrow end, roll tightly. Pinch the ends of the roll together and fold about 2 inches under on each side. Place in pan, seam-side down, cover, and let rise in a warm place until very light (about 1 hour).

Bake until richly browned (about 35 minutes), let sit in the pan for 5 minutes, then run a knife around the loaf and carefully turn it out. Cool on a rack placed over a pan to catch any sugar that drips out.

TOASTING BREAD

Makes 2 loaves

Toasting is used here as an adjective, not a gerund. This is "bread for toasting." It resulted when I became infuriated after toasting various samples of corn bread and never being able to extricate the crumbling pieces from the toaster. So I decided to make a bread that is as dense as corn bread, but can still be sliced and toasted in a regular pop-up toaster. It's a nice, heavy (as opposed to a light and fluffy) whole grain bread that can be sliced very thin if you wish. It is also good untoasted.

This recipe is based on one that was published in *Sunset* magazine more than twenty years ago. It was included in a wonderful article about variations on a basic whole grain bread. To my mind, anyone starting a bakery that just offered the breads from that article would make a fortune. The article was called "So you'd like to try a whole grain bread," and it appeared in the Western edition in March, 1968.

Here's one thing I love about this dough. Normally, it doesn't matter how careful I am about rolling dough up, it always seems to want to distort itself or unroll. This recipe solves that problem. When the dough is properly rolled up, it fits perfectly in the pan and so it doesn't unroll.

I really like the bread to rise a lot in the pan. In this, I think I am more daring than are many bread bakers. Some books warn you that whole grains are heavy and should not over-rise. But I tend to let it go long and only twice in about 3,000 times have I had over-risen dough.

It is important to cool the bread thoroughly, preferably overnight, before slicing it. Whole grain breads tend to be somewhat gummy when they are sliced warm.

2 packages dry yeast (check the expiration date to avoid problems)	3 Tbsp. vegetable oil
	½ cup honey
2 cups warm water (about 110°)	1½ cups cornmeal
1 cup nonfat dry milk powder	1½ cups toasted wheat germ
2½ tsp. salt	1½ cups whole wheat flour
About 3½ cups white flour	

Dissolve the yeast in ¼ cup of the warm water and stir. Set aside for 5 minutes until foamy.

In a large bowl, combine the remaining warm water, dry milk powder, salt, white flour, oil, and honey and beat for 5 minutes with a heavy wooden spoon until strands of batter start to pull away from the sides of the bowl. Gradually beat in the cornmeal, wheat germ, and as much whole wheat flour as you can add.

Turn the dough out onto a lightly floured surface and begin to knead, adding the rest of the whole wheat flour if the dough is too sticky. Knead for a full 5 minutes after the last addition of flour. The dough will be smooth and elastic. If it seems to be a little too sticky, cover it with a dry towel and leave it alone for about 5 minutes.

smoke when the dial has been set on "Dark" and it shouldn't have been.

Usually, our toast is served with melted butter on it, but of course there are customers who want it dry. We will make toast to any desired color (more than a few people ask for it virtually burned) but thankfully, most people happily accept our standard for how done toast should be (golden brown). All we need is one more major complication at our toast station. It's a little soap opera every weekend.

Place the dough in a large greased or oiled bowl, grease the top of the dough, and cover the bowl. Let it rise in a warm place (about 85°) for about 1½ hours, or until almost doubled. Punch down, turn out, and knead a few times to remove air bubbles.

Divide the dough in half and form each half into a 5- by 9-inch rectangle, either using a rolling pin or the heel of your hand. Starting from the 5-inch end, roll the dough up loosely and place, seam-side down, into a greased 4- by 8-inch loaf pan, making sure the ends of the dough touch the sides of the pan. Repeat with the other half and a second loaf pan. Cover and let rise in a warm place until almost doubled (about 50 to 60 minutes).

Preheat the oven to 350° and brush the tops of the loaves with melted butter. Bake for about 45 minutes until the loaves are richly browned on top and bottom. Cover with foil if top appears too brown. Turn out and let cool on racks. Cool completely, preferably overnight, before slicing for toast.

MANDELBROT

Makes 3 to 4 dozen slices

For those who do not want a hearty meal in the morning, *Mandelbrot* and a cup of coffee or tea may be a good way to start the day. *Mandelbrot* means almond bread, but this recipe can be made with hazelnuts, in which case the name becomes *Haselnussbrot*. Nowadays it seems as if everybody and her sister is making this sort of confection and its Italian cousin, *biscotti*. It is a cookie that is baked twice: first in a loaf form, then cut and baked again as slices. (*Biscotti* means "twice baked.")

The American Dental Association encourages the dunking of *Mandelbrot*; it is so hard, teeth have been known to chip. You can be creative or outrageous in the things you dunk it into, besides the obvious coffee or tea: hot chocolate, chocolate *sauce*, hot milk and honey.

This recipe is my mom's and it's a good one. The finished product will last almost forever in an airtight container, if well hidden.

3½ cups white flour	½ cup corn oil
2 tsp. baking powder	2 tsp. vanilla extract
¼ tsp. salt	½ tsp. almond extract
3 eggs	1 cup chopped toasted almonds
1 cup sugar	or hazelnuts

Preheat the oven to 350°. Sift the flour with the baking powder and salt and set aside. Beat the eggs and add the sugar gradually, beating until the batter is thick. Add the oil, vanilla and almond extracts, then the dry ingredients and nuts. Stir to combine. Divide the dough into 3 equal portions. Sprinkle flour onto a pastry board and knead one portion of the dough for 2 or 3 minutes, until smooth and not sticky. Add a little more flour if needed.

Shape the dough into a loaf about 9 inches long, ¾ of an inch high, and 2½ inches wide. Traditionally, the loaf has a slightly arched or curved top. Place across the width of a greased 9- by 13-inch pan. Repeat with the 2 remaining pieces of dough. Bake for 30 to 35 minutes.

Remove the pan from the oven but *do not turn off oven*. Immediately remove the loaves and, with a sharp knife, cut into slices no more than ½ an inch thick. Sometimes they are cut diagonally. Lay the slices on ungreased 10- by 15-inch cookie sheets, return to the oven, and bake for about 12 to 15 minutes, until golden brown. During the baking, turn the slices over when one side is brown. Remove from oven and let cool in pan.

FOODS OUT OF SEASON

You can often find fresh, or at least apparently fresh produce completely out of season, either because it comes from the Southern Hemisphere, or perhaps from greenhouses. But you always pay a premium in price—I remember $5-a-pound asparagus last winter—and often in quality as well. Since there are always *some* in-season fruits and vegetables available, I generally advocate using them. Also, many out-of-season fruits and vegetables come from countries where a lot of pesticides are used that are not permitted in this country.

1. Don't worry about
the exact measurements
of ingredients. Bread is
forgiving.

2. Use a much big-
ger bread bowl than you
really need.

3. Accept the indis-
putable fact that most
breads take about four
hours to make, from start
to finish, and there's nothing you can do about it.

4. Plan for other ac-
tivities to do during the
bread making's down
time.

5. Learn to stir with
the other arm or you will
end up with one arm like
Arnold Schwarzenegger's
and one arm like Sissy
Spacek's.

6. Commit yourself
to a clean-as-you-go
policy.

BILL BROWN'S FIVE-FLOUR BROWN BREAD

Makes 6 loaves

Bill Brown is a Canadian man who kidnapped Janet McCulloch, one of our best waitresses. Well, actually, he married her a few years ago in Canada, moved to the Mendocino area, and recently took her back to Victoria with him. Our loss; Canada's gain. He is an English and math teacher, a poetry fiend (write me for details on Bill's patented poetry memorization course), a carpenter, a plumber, an electrician, and—perhaps most important—he bakes delicious breads.

As I was working on this book, he would present me every few days with a loaf of his magical bread, always asking if I were sure I *really* wanted it. He was genuinely concerned that I would spurn any bread that didn't come from our own then-brand-new wood-fired brick oven. Ha! I would delightedly cut a few slices from his hearty loaves, toast them, and dine contentedly with a cup of tea. They nourished me and kept me going for hours at a time.

Bill has decided to share his recipe with the world and you are so lucky.

2 cups warm water
2 Tbsp. sugar, honey, or molasses
2 Tbsp. dry yeast (check expiration date)
5 cups flour (not white), grain, and/or cereal: 1 cup each of any 5 of these: rye, whole wheat, soy, seven-grain, bulgur, granola, Grape-Nuts, wheat germ, Cheerios, All-Bran, Shredded Wheat, etc.
1 cup sunflower seeds
2 Tbsp. salt
2 cups raisins (optional)
4 cups hot water
About 13 cups white flour

In a medium-sized bowl, mix the warm water and sugar. Add the yeast and stir. Set aside in a warm place for 10 minutes.

In a large bowl, place the 5 cups of whatever ingredient(s) you have chosen from the list of possibilities, the sunflower seeds, salt, and the raisins if you are including them. Add the hot water and stir with a wooden spoon until the mixture resembles porridge. Let cool until lukewarm. Stir the yeast mixture and add it to the porridge, mixing thoroughly. Gradually begin adding the white flour, stirring until it becomes impossible to do so any longer.

Turn the sticky dough onto a floured board, scraping out the bowl thoroughly. Knead in as much flour as it takes to make the dough smooth and no longer sticky. You must knead for 5 minutes after the last addition of flour. When ready, the dough will be elastic and springy, with air bubbles visible under the surface, and you will be tired.

Place the dough in a large, lightly greased bowl and turn it to grease the entire surface of the dough. Cover with a clean dry cloth and let rise in a warm place until doubled (about 1 hour). Punch it down and let it rise until doubled again (about 45 minutes). Punch it down, turn it out, and knead a few more times.

Divide the dough into 6 equal pieces and form them into fat 8-inch-long cigars. Place in greased 4- by 8-inch bread pans, making sure that the ends of the dough touch the ends of the pan. Cover the pans and let the loaves rise until the dough has almost doubled (about 45 minutes).

Preheat oven to 375°. Bake for 40 minutes on the lower rack, until tops and bottoms are richly browned. Tap on the bottoms; they should sound hollow. If not, return to the oven for another 5 minutes and check again. Turn out and cool thoroughly on racks. Freeze whatever you don't plan to use within 2 days.

POPPY-SEED YEAST BREAD

Serves 8 to 10

I like poppy seeds a lot. My father is Hungarian and, when I was little, he would take me to ethnic bakeries to seek out *Mohnkuchen*, a traditional Eastern European poppy-seed cake. I made up this bread recipe as an excuse for the filling, a poppy-seed paste that traditionally fills pastries in Hungarian, Austrian, and German recipes.

I like the shape that this bread forms, with the very attractive yet very simple-to-do braid on the top. Few people make this sort of yeast bread or coffee cake often. But it is easy and makes a fine presentation.

BREAD
1½ Tbsp. dry yeast (check the
    expiration date)
¼ cup warm water
¼ cup warm milk
½ tsp. salt
¼ cup sugar
1 egg
¼ cup butter, at room
    temperature
3 cups unsifted white flour
Egg wash: 1 egg white beaten
    with 1 tsp. water
3 Tbsp. sliced almonds

POPPY-SEED FILLING
¾ cup poppy seeds
¾ cup whole almonds or
    hazelnuts
½ cup white sugar
⅓ cup milk
1 tsp. grated lemon peel
1 Tbsp. lemon juice
3 Tbsp. butter

Dissolve the yeast in water with a pinch of sugar. Let it stand for 5 minutes, then stir and blend in the milk, salt, sugar, egg, and butter. Gradually beat in about 2½ cups of the flour to make a soft dough.

Turn the dough out onto a lightly floured board and, adding the remaining ½ cup flour as necessary, knead until it is smooth and satiny, about 5 minutes. Turn the dough over in a greased bowl, cover, and let it rise in a warm place until doubled (about 1½ hours).

To make the Poppy-Seed Filling, combine the poppy seeds and almonds or hazelnuts in a blender or food processor and blend until the mixture is the consistency of cornmeal. In a small pan, combine with the rest of the filling ingredients and cook over low heat, stirring until the mixture boils and thickens (about 10 minutes). Cool.

When the dough has risen sufficiently, punch it down. On a flat, greased sideless 10- by 15-inch pan, roll the dough out to cover the entire surface. Mark the dough lightly into 3 lengthwise sections. Spread the poppy-seed filling over the center third of the dough. Cut about 10 diagonal strips in each of the 2 outer sections of the dough, scoring at an angle from the outside almost as far as the filling. Fold these strips up over the filling, alternately, first one side, then the other: a braided effect.

Brush the loaf with the egg wash and sprinkle top with almonds. Let the loaf rise uncovered in a warm place until it has almost doubled (about 45 minutes).

Bake at 350° for 30 minutes. Cool on a rack.

CORN BREAD

Cornmeal appears on our menus almost daily, in pancakes, waffles, breads, or entrées. One of the things I love about corn bread is that it is good to eat by itself, but it also is a wonderful starting place for developing other recipes and dishes. You can invent little dishes around it really quickly. Cut a piece in half, melt cheese on it, and cover it with Salsa (see page 140). And then there's Tex-Mex Cornbread Pudding (see page 156).

⅓ cup white sugar	½ tsp. baking soda
½ cup vegetable oil	¾ tsp. salt
2 eggs, beaten	1½ cups cornmeal
1⅓ cups unsifted white flour	1 cup buttermilk
2½ tsp. baking powder	

Preheat the oven to 400°. Blend together the sugar, oil, and eggs. Sift together the flour, baking powder, soda, and salt. Add about one-third of the dry ingredients to the liquid ingredients, then one-third of the buttermilk, one-third of the dry, and so on, until it is all blended together.

Pour into a greased 9-inch square pan and bake for about 30 minutes, until top is lightly browned.

POLISH RAISIN BREAD

Makes 3 loaves

This traditional Polish bread is quite rich, with a light and elegant cakelike texture, especially when toasted and smothered in butter. The dough is extremely satisfying to knead; you may find yourself reluctant to stop. In the restaurant, I made French toast with it and everyone went wild. If there are leftovers, it freezes well.

The recipe comes from my friend and the manager of the Cafe Beaujolais Bakery, Lorraine Ardaiz. She and her friend, Cove Norvell, bake this bread frequently, but, as with many cooks, it was really hard for them to come up with specific quantities of ingredients until I twisted their various arms for the recipe.

My suggestion that we add cinnamon was met with horror: "But that's not Polish!" Lorraine shrieked. Hey, am I an iconoclast or what? I broke with tradition and added lemon zest, and you should too. Just don't tell Lorraine.

2 packages dry yeast (check the expiration date)	2 tsp. salt
½ cup warm water	1 cup white sugar
1 cup lukewarm milk	7 eggs
2 tsp. finely grated lemon rind	About 9 cups white flour
½ cup butter, softened	1¾ cups raisins

Dissolve the yeast in the water in a small bowl. Stir and set in a warm place for 5 minutes.

In a large mixing bowl, place the milk, lemon rind, butter, salt, sugar, and 6 of the eggs and whisk to combine. Whisk in the yeast and then 3 cups of the flour. Beat for two minutes or until smooth. Using a heavy wooden spoon instead of the wisk, add about 3½ cups of flour gradually. When the dough is too stiff to beat with spoon, turn it out onto a lightly floured board and knead for 10 minutes, adding flour as necessary.

Sprinkle the raisins over surface and knead them in.

Place the dough in a large greased bowl and turn it so that all sides are shiny. Cover with a dry dish towel and place in a warm place. Let it rise until doubled (about 2 hours).

Then preheat the oven to 350°. Punch the dough down and turn it out. Knead a few times to remove air bubbles. Divide the dough evenly into 3 pieces and form into loaves.

Place each loaf into a 4- by 8-inch bread pan. Cover with dish towels and let them rise in a warm place until doubled (about 1½ hours). Gently brush the tops with the remaining egg, beaten, and bake for about 35 to 45 minutes, or until the loaves are richly browned on the bottom as well as the top. (If the top appears to be browning excessively, cover loosely with a sheet of foil.) Remove the loaves from the pans when done, and let cool on a rack, on their sides.

COFFEE CAKES

YEASTED APPLE-RAISIN CAKE

Serves 8 to 10

An antique organic apple and pear orchard lies in the meadow east of our house in Mendocino, and every September, as the fruit ripens, Chris and I are faced with the task of figuring out what to do with about 2,000 pounds of fruit. Our Apples Butter (the plural refers to the many varieties that go into it), sold through Cafe Beaujolais Bakery, takes care of about two-thirds of the crop. Made without any sugar, the thick rich spicy spread propels toast into a new dimension.

The rest of the fruit finds its way into many different breakfast items and desserts: sautéed apple slices, lightly seasoned with cinnamon and nutmeg, transform pancakes, waffles, and muffins.

A few years ago, I was asked to do a demonstration at the Culinary Carnival in San Francisco, which is a yearly fund-raising event for Children's Garden in Marin. I decided to create a recipe for an apple cake, but every time I tried it, something was slightly wrong. Refining a recipe in front of 400 people was a bit scary, but all went well, and this recipe is the result.

What's nice about this pastry is that you can make the filling part the day before, and refrigerate it; then the next morning, you can get up, make the batter, and finish it off.

Use Pippin or Granny Smith apples. At home, our apples have old-fashioned and romantic names such as Tompkins, King and Winter Banana, but we're not exactly sure what they correspond to at the market. But fresh locally-grown apples always seem to taste better and their fragrance is like perfume.

First Aid Warning: Pay extremely close attention when working with hot sugar syrup. If you do get any on the skin, immerse the burned area immediately in cold water.

DOUGH
2 tsp. dry yeast (check the expiration date)
1 tsp. white sugar
2 Tbsp. warm water
1/2 cup warm milk
3 large eggs
1 3/4 cups white flour
3/4 tsp. salt
5 Tbsp. softened, unsalted butter

FILLING
3 1/2 lb. tart apples, peeled, cored, and quartered
2 Tbsp. lemon juice
3/4 cup brandy
2 1/2 cups white sugar
1/2 cup water
1/2 cup raisins

TOPPING
Very lightly sweetened whipped cream or Crème Fraîche

Dissolve the yeast and sugar in warm water, stir, and set aside for a few minutes.

In the bowl of an electric blender, place the milk, eggs, flour, and salt. Beat until blended and add the softened and foamy yeast. Beat for 4 more minutes, add the butter and beat for another minute until blended. With a rubber spatula, scrape the sides down and cover the bowl with plastic wrap. Let the

CONTINUED FROM BOOK ONE

People ask me questions about some unresolved matters mentioned in my first book, *Cafe Beaujolais.* Here are three of them.

We were considering instituting a no-smoking policy, and we have done so. The nonsmokers are grateful, and the smokers have been good about stepping out onto the deck.

We no longer accept credit cards. We were, infrequently, plagued with bad credit cards and, more frequently, with lots of extra paperwork and a not insignificant service charge. So we decided: To heck with it and now take no plastic at all.

Doug Chouteau, a customer who warranted an entire page, was not offended by my observations. He has moved away from Mendocino, but he's been back a few times.

In my first book, I described myself as someone who is very relatable-to. It's true, but it has its limits. One day, after dealing with a great many annoying people, I just wanted to announce, "I am *not* Margaret Fox. I cannot deal with all of this *relating to people,* because it is very tiring." Sometimes I wonder if the relating just takes me away from the real things I do and which attracted people in the first place.

What *are* the real things I do? I cook and I help organize things. Last August, several members of the staff got sick and one person left to have a baby. Suddenly I was working in the kitchen for about sixty hours a week. I was like a pig in mud. It was just like the early days of the restaurant: work hard, go home exhausted, go to bed, get up, and cook. It was really great fun . . . for a while.

But change is essential for growth. I have no interest in starting a new career at this time, or opening branches, or franchising. Change for me must be within the context of what I have been doing. For instance, we've just built a brick oven next to the restaurant, to use for baking breads and pizzas. It was good for me to be able to engage my brain in thinking about and planning that major undertaking with Chris and Tricia. I needed that new project. There is something about dealing only with the practical and the tangible and ignoring the transcendent that I find somewhat stifling after a while.

dough rise in a warm place until doubled (about 1½ hours). While the dough is rising, proceed with recipe (unless you are making it the night before and are planning to refrigerate it).

Mix together the apples, lemon juice, and brandy. Set aside. In a heavy-bottomed pan over low heat, mix together the sugar and water until the sugar dissolves. Bring to a boil and continue cooking over medium heat, using a brush dipped in water to wash down the sides of the pan to dissolve any crystals that form. When the sugar and water are a rich caramel color, turn off the heat and add the apples, lemon juice, and brandy, taking great care to protect yourself from any splashing or spattering bits of the incredibly hot sugar syrup. Stir to blend well, cover, and cook at a low heat for 5 minutes to soften the apples slightly without letting much liquid evaporate.

Pour the apple compote into a lightly buttered 9- by 13-inch pan. Stir in the raisins. Let the mixture cool to room temperature (about 45 minutes). If impatient, you can hurry this along by placing the pan in the refrigerator.

When the dough has doubled, beat it down with a wooden spoon and spread it over the room-temperature compote. Use a spatula to spread evenly. The layer will be very thin; you may see some little holes, but that's OK.

Preheat the oven to 350°. Let the cake rise in a warm place until the dough is puffy (about 45 minutes). Don't cover with plastic wrap because the batter will stick and make a mess. Carefully place in the oven and bake for about 35 minutes, until golden brown.

Remove from the oven and let the pan cool on a wire rack for 10 minutes. With great care, invert the cake onto a large flat pan or plate. Serve with very lightly sweetened whipped cream or *crème fraîche*.

Morning Timetable

5:30 AM Start fire
Pull all breads _____, proof
Portion levain _____, proof
Portion batard _____, proof
Portion dinner _____, proof
1st roll batard, proof
1st roll dinner, proof
Roll levain to banneton, proof
2nd roll batard, cloth, proof
2nd roll dinner, banneton, proof
_____ refresh starter

6:30 AM Pizza prep, tend fire
(Try to keep brust oven temp—usually well—below 600°)

7:00 AM Portion fougasse (14oz), proof
7:15 Add nuts to hazel (in Hobie!)
7:10 Shape focaccia

7:30 AM Piece Dough; rake (metal, wood & brush)
mop oven

8:00 AM Pizza prep;
7:15 Portion herb (14oz), 1st roll   520-540
8:30 AM Load focaccia & batards
Steam,
Shape & banneton herb;

8:40-8:50 AM 8:50-900 AM Unload focaccia & batards   500-510
900-940 AM Load dinner & levain   510
2 steams (5 min interval)

BUTTERMILK-CINNAMON COFFEE CAKE

Makes 12 servings

No one can claim to be a member of the Cafe Beaujolais Fan Club without devouring at least two pieces of this addictive coffee cake. Our staff renews its membership regularly. We've actually tried to stop making it, but our customers won't let us, so now it has become a permanent fixture on the menu.

2¼ cups white flour	1 cup chopped walnuts or
½ tsp. salt	pecans
2 tsp. cinnamon	1 tsp. baking soda
¼ tsp. ginger	1 tsp. baking powder
1 cup brown sugar	1 egg, beaten
¾ cup white sugar	1 cup buttermilk
¾ cup corn oil	

Mix together in a large bowl the flour, salt, 1 tsp. of the cinnamon, ginger, both sugars, and corn oil. Remove ¾ cup of this mixture, and to it add the nuts and the remaining teaspoon of cinnamon. Mix well, and set aside to use as a topping.

To the remaining batter, add the baking soda, baking powder, egg, and buttermilk. Mix to combine all ingredients. Small lumps in the batter are OK.

Pour the batter into a well-greased 9- by 13- by 2-inch pan. Sprinkle the topping mixture evenly over the surface. Bake at 350° for 40 to 45 minutes.

In 1984, Tricia, our manager, and I realized that we weren't sure whether to offer dinner that year. We'd had our ups and downs with dinner service. Because we served dinner only during the summer, it didn't pay to keep a dinner chef around in the off-season, so we had a new chef almost every year.

We finally decided *not* to do dinner, a decision that caused much distress among those staff members who were expecting to work at dinnertime. But I felt good about the decision. It is quite luxurious to think, when you are a morning person such as I am, that your workday is officially over at about three in the afternoon. Adding dinner is like adding a whole new business on top of everything else that's going on, and life begins to take on a 24-hour-a-day quality.

Lo and behold, just at this time, one of the people who were going to lose their evening jobs noticed an advertisement in our local weekly, the *Mendocino Beacon*. It was placed by a European-trained chef who was looking for a job in Mendocino and included a long-distance number. I thought to myself, why bother. Everybody who has had a meal at the airport restaurant in London calls himself a "European-trained" chef. But, what the heck, let's just see.

I phoned the number and left a message. We finally spoke, and he sounded vaguely OK, so we made an appointment for an interview a week

YOGURT COFFEE CAKE

Serves 12

This recipe has been in my files for so long that I honestly can't remember where it came from. The original called for sour cream, but I found I can substitute low-fat yogurt without any detectable change whatsoever. And when I added the chocolate chips, the entire staff descended upon the pan, which is always a good sign. Sometimes I think we could have saved a lot on typesetting for this book by saying, on page one, "Optional: chocolate chips may be added to every recipe."

1¼ cups yogurt	TOPPING
1¼ tsp. baking soda, sifted	½ cup chopped nuts
½ cup butter, softened	1 tsp. cinnamon
1¼ cups white sugar	⅓ cup brown sugar
2 eggs, beaten	
1¾ cups white flour	
1¾ tsp. baking powder	
⅔ cup chocolate chips (optional)	

Preheat the oven to 350°.

In a large bowl, mix together the yogurt and soda and set aside.

Cream together the butter, sugar, and eggs until fluffy. In a separate bowl, sift together the flour and baking powder, and add to the butter mixture and blend. Quickly stir in the yogurt and soda.

Pour into a greased 9- by 13-inch pan. If you are using chocolate chips, sprinkle them evenly on the surface and press them lightly into batter. Combine the topping ingredients and sprinkle it evenly on surface. Bake for about 40 to 45 minutes, until it tests done with a toothpick.

later. During that ensuing week, Tricia and I came to the decision that we absolutely didn't want to do dinners, no matter what. This was going to be the year that we had time to recover and renew ourselves. "What about that guy coming up for an interview?" Tricia asked. "Oh, heck, let him come; maybe we can help him find a job somewhere else."

So Chris Kump came, and we had a pleasant talk for a couple of hours. He really *was* a European-trained chef, whose father ran a well-known cooking school in New York. He had grown up working with the likes of James Beard, and Julia Child, and Simone Beck. He had worked at excellent restaurants in New York and Paris. We knew a lot of the same people, and it was a very easy conversation.

When he left, Tricia and I looked at each other and both thought, "How can we let this person go? He would be so right for us." We called him up and told him that we wanted him to make a test meal for seven or eight of us on April 28th, 1984, the seventh anniversary of the restaurant. Chris arrived and took over the kitchen. He seemed to be doing a dozen things at once. I went in and offered to help by making bread, but he said no, he had that under control too.

We proceeded to have an astounding meal. There was a scallop and avocado *seviche* beautifully plated; an incredible ragout that included artichoke hearts, and some

RACHEL'S VERSION OF THE ANCHORAGE PETROLEUM WIVES' CLUB COFFEE CAKE

Makes 2 cakes, each serving 12

This delicious coffee cake appears frequently at Rachel's Bed and Breakfast, a particularly beautiful inn two miles south of Mendocino. It is owned and operated by the talented Rachel Binah, who is a leader in the Ocean Sanctuary movement fighting *for* permanent protection for the ocean and *against* oil exploration and drilling off the coast. It appeals to her sense of irony to offer this cake, which she first encountered while visiting her sister in Alaska.

The cake itself is a yeasted coffee cake with your choice of two fillings. The way the strips of dough are folded into a lattice pattern makes a very attractive presentation. The cake may be frozen when assembled but not yet risen. Defrost in the refrigerator overnight, then bake in the morning.

2 packages yeast (check the
    expiration date)
½ cup warm water
¼ cup sugar
5 cups white flour
1 tsp. salt
1 cup butter
8 oz. cream cheese
1 egg
1 tsp. vanilla extract
1 cup buttermilk

APRICOT-ALMOND OR
PRUNE-PECAN FILLING
Each enough for 2 cakes
2¼ cups dried, pitted apricots
    or prunes
¾ cup sugar
1½ cups orange juice
1½ cups chopped nuts
ICING
½ cup powdered sugar mixed
    with
1 Tbsp. lemon juice

In a small bowl, sprinkle the yeast over the warm water, add a pinch of the sugar, and stir. Set aside for 5 minutes to proof.

In a large bowl, stir together the flour, the rest of the sugar, and salt and, using a pastry blender, cut in the butter and cream cheese. You can also place the dry ingredients into the bowl of a food processor and cut in the butter and cream cheese with the metal S-blade.

Stir in the egg, vanilla, and buttermilk and knead for 5 minutes on a lightly floured surface. Place the dough in a greased bowl and turn to grease the top. Cover the bowl with a dry dish towel and let it rise for about 1¼ hours, or until doubled.

Prepare the filling by chopping the fruit and mixing with the sugar. Place in a small pot with juice and cook until the juice is almost evaporated. Add the nuts and set aside to cool.

very exotic seafood. Dessert was extraordinary: apple slices that had been sprinkled with sugar, baked, and then spread out in a fan with cinnamon ice cream that Chris had made. He didn't know what a chocoholic I am, but that night it didn't matter. This is still one of my all-time favorite desserts.

Each course was treated separately, as a star, rather than as one of a number of elements in the meal as a whole, so the combined effect was far richer than any meal you'd ever want to serve to the public. We could not have been more impressed. I had not had sauces like that since the time friends and I took a loaf of French bread and cleaned out the saucepans at the Great Chefs of France cooking school.

Of course we hired him . . . and then, somehow, during the next three or four months, we wound up falling in love. We worked so hard during this period, all the more so because it was Chris's first time at managing a kitchen. That summer had more than its share of problems and overambitious plans, and we really didn't end up making any money. But it was clear that he had an extraordinary talent.

Why, I hear you asking, did he advertise up here in the first place? His mother had happened to visit Mendocino the previous year and found it to be the wonderfully charming place that it is. She knew her son had always wanted to live near the water. So she suggested to him that he check it out. He came on an exploratory trip and ate at a number of restaurants, excluding Cafe Beaujolais for some reason, and decided that this could be the place. So he ran the ad to test the waters, as it were.

In October, to my sorrow, he left to work at a restaurant in southwest France, the Hôtel de France in Auch, run by André Daguin. We tentatively planned to meet in Paris in about two and a half months time, but he didn't know about my acute fear of flying. Somehow I flew over there, lured by romance, and my first trip to Europe, and the prospect of two months of magnificent eating. We had a wonderful time, eating our way through Europe, from three-star restaurants to country cafés at which the entire meal, including wine and yogurt dessert, cost two dollars.

When we returned to Mendocino, we bought a house together, on three and a half acres. We are still living here, with our three large dogs, twenty-one fruit trees, and an overwhelming garden.

We got married in January, 1988. We spend much of our time working together, dealing fairly well with all the problems inherent in a relationship that requires us to work with each other all day and then try to lead a private life after hours. I wouldn't recommend it, but I will say that it poses some interesting problems.

Punch the dough down and divide it into 2 pieces. Using 2 large greased cookie sheets, roll each piece of dough out into a rectangle, measuring about 12- by 15- by ¼-inch, directly onto the sheets. Spread the filling evenly along the middle third of the dough.

Cut the dough into about 20 strips on each side of the filling, at an angle from the outside to just where the filling begins. Fold a strip from the left side over the center filling, then one from the right side, and so on, making a lattice pattern of the strips.

Cover each coffee cake and let it rise until doubled (about 1 hour). Preheat the oven to 350° and then bake for about 55 to 60 minutes, or until golden brown. Remove from oven, let cool for 10 minutes, then drizzle with the icing.

STREUSEL-CARAMEL COFFEE CAKE

Serves 9 to 12

Recipe-testing can be a frustrating experience. Sometimes the recipe must be tried over and over again, with slight variations, until it reaches the desired form. One gauge of the success of a recipe is the speed with which the finished product disappears. This coffee cake clocked in at about seven minutes.

This recipe is unusual in that the caramels are actually in the batter, rather than being a part of the streusel or the topping. I'm not a fan of overly gooey toppings, so I prefer the caramels inside, where they all melt together. They disappear from sight, but the taste is quite wonderful.

My friend Barbara Holzrichter founded and operates the smallest licensed candy factory in California—a little gem of an operation up in the Berkeley hills. Her buttercream caramels are, as they are advertised to be, the melt-in-your-mouth kind; not the stick-to-your-teeth kind. Because they are melted in this recipe, ordinary store-bought caramels will do (but you can get the real thing from us by mail; see page xv). If you use store-bought caramels, soften them first by unwrapping them and placing on a pan in a 350° oven for about 5 minutes.

BATTER	STREUSEL MIXTURE
3/4 cup sugar	1 cup brown sugar
1/4 cup butter, softened	1/4 cup white flour
1 egg	2 tsp. cinnamon
1/2 cup milk	1/2 cup butter, melted
1 1/2 cups white flour	1 cup chopped walnuts
2 tsp. baking powder	
1/2 tsp. salt	
9 caramels	

Preheat the oven to 350°. Grease an 8-inch square pan.

Beat together the sugar, butter, and egg. Stir in the milk. Sift together the flour, baking powder, and salt, then blend into the butter mixture.

Spread two-thirds of the batter in the pan. One by one pull the caramels into 4-inch ribbons and then press them into the batter with your fingers. Place them at regular intervals. Mix together the streusel ingredients and sprinkle it evenly over the batter. Cover with the remaining batter. Bake for 40 to 45 minutes, or until a toothpick stuck into the center comes out clean.

ALMOND- OR CHOCOLATE-FILLED COFFEE CAKE

Serves 8

Another variation on the theme . . . and another opportunity to start the day with some chocolate.

8 oz. blanched almonds
½ cup sugar
1 tsp. lemon juice
1 tsp. almond extract
⅓ cup softened butter
2 tsp. white flour
1 tsp. grated lemon peel (packed)
3 Tbsp. dry crumbs (fine dry bread, butter cookie, or graham cracker)

1 egg
2 oz. chocolate chips (optional)
Half of Basic Sweet-Roll Dough recipe (page 51) made with **lemon** peel instead of **orange** peel
1 Tbsp. melted butter
Glaze made from 1 beaten egg and 1 Tbsp. milk

Preheat the oven to 350°. Place the almonds and sugar into the bowl of a food processor fitted with a metal S-blade and process until the mixture resembles coarse meal. Add the lemon juice, almond extract, softened butter, flour, lemon peel, crumbs, egg, and chocolate chips and process until mixture is combined. (If you are using chocolate, little lumps may remain.) Set aside.

On a lightly floured board, roll the dough into a 10- by 16-inch rectangle. The dough will be elastic and difficult to roll out. If it fights you every inch of the way, cover with a clean, dry cloth and let it rest for about 5 minutes. After this wait, you should have no problem in rolling the dough to the proper size.

Brush with melted butter and spread the filling evenly over the surface except for a 1-inch-wide strip along one of the 10-inch sides. Starting with the other 10-inch side, roll the dough towards you as tightly as is reasonable, taking care not to squoosh the filling out of the roll. Pinch the seam and place roll, seam-side down, on a greased 10- by 15-inch baking sheet.

While the roll is lying flat on the sheet, bend it around into a circle (like a giant doughnut) and pinch the ends together. Holding a knife vertically, cut from the outside to the inside, about three-fourths of the way through the circle, making 11 incisions (see illustrations below).

Step 1   Step 2   Step 3

Cover with a clean dry dish towel and let the loaf rise in a warm place until puffy and about doubled in size. Brush gently with the glaze, taking care not to let it run onto the pan. Bake for 25 to 30 minutes, or until richly browned. Remove from the oven. Leave the coffee cake on the pan and set on a rack to cool.

CHOCOLATE COFFEE CAKE

Serves 12 generously

This is a coffee cake that I've made over the years for my chocoholic friends. Nowadays I make it with yogurt instead of sour cream and the results are perfectly respectable.

I like to think of this cake as having everything sweet you've ever liked in one dish. It has chocolate; it has apricots; it has almonds. What with chocolate chips *and* cocoa, there's no question about how chocolatey it is. It is definitely chocolatey. The chips pretty much melt into it, so there aren't discrete chips left when you eat it, just more chocolate in the cake. It's also very elegant—the sort of thing you could serve at a dignified tea.

I'm always being urged by the staff to make this more often, but I don't. This is one of those recipes that are really easy when you're just making one at home, but a tremendous bother to do in restaurant-sized quantities, because we can't just make one big one; we have to make a dozen small ones. It winds up being a huge mess, and I'm up to my shoulders in batter, ready to lay down my spatula and go home.

I suggest that this cake be made in a Bundt pan, a round pan with decorations on the outside. But you can also do it in a regular 9- by 13-inch coffee cake pan. It will taste the same, of course; it just won't look as attractive. But since it will probably be around for about nine minutes anyway, what's the difference?

And if you're still worried about all this sweetness early in the day, think of it as a mixture of apricots, yogurt, and almonds. The smidgen of chocolate is only superficial. Maybe we should call it Chocolate Health Coffee Cake.

NUT FILLING	CAKE BATTER
¾ cup light brown sugar	2¾ cups white flour
1 Tbsp. cinnamon	1½ tsp. double-acting baking
2 Tbsp. powdered instant coffee	powder
3 Tbsp. chopped dried apricots	1½ tsp. baking soda
2 Tbsp. unsweetened cocoa	½ tsp. salt
1 cup coarsely chopped toasted	¾ cup softened butter
almonds	1½ cups white sugar
¼ cup chocolate chips	1 tsp. vanilla extract
	3 eggs
	2 cups yogurt

Preheat the oven to 350°. Mix together all the ingredients for the nut filling and set aside.

Sift together the flour, baking powder, baking soda, and salt and set aside. In the bowl of an electric mixer, beat the butter until very light and fluffy. Add the sugar and vanilla and beat for 2 minutes. Add the eggs and continue beating for another 2 minutes. This mixture must be very smooth.

Gradually add the flour mixture, alternating with the yogurt, and beat only until the mixture is smooth after each addition.

DIVISION OF LABOR

At the restaurant Chris is usually entirely responsible for the dinners. Occasionally, when we do differ, I find myself defending, not my own opinion, but the position of the restaurant, as if I were the Cafe's alter ego or its advocate. "Wait a minute," I think, "This *is* my business and I do know something about it."

For instance, last December, Chris decided that he wanted to offer a Thai-based New Year's Eve dinner. After I heard the whole menu, I felt it just wasn't right. Thai restaurants have become commonplace in the San Francisco area. Why would people want to drive all that way just for another Thai meal, no matter how delicious? Also there was the matter of economics. You can get a very good Thai meal for ten or twelve dollars a person. Would anyone pay forty dollars for a Thai feast?

We had a few somewhat strained conversations about this. I fully supported his wish to be creative and break new ground but, when Cafe Beaujolais is involved, it is as if the restaurant casts the deciding vote. We ended up doing an extremely elegant French dinner, which was a grand success.

Butter a 10-inch Bundt pan or 9- by 13-inch coffee cake pan generously and pour the batter and filling into the pan in the following way: batter, filling, batter, filling, batter.

Bake for about 1 hour and 10 minutes. Test to make sure the cake is completely baked. Cool on a rack for 10 minutes, then turn out with great care.

To serve, sift powdered sugar lightly over the top of the cake. Best served warm.

PANCAKES, WAFFLES & FRENCH TOAST

HEALTHY PANCAKES *Makes 12 to 15 pancakes*

Pancakes with yeast may strike you as being very time consuming, because you have to wait for the batter to rise before the pancakes can be made. If you make the batter the night before, the only thing you'll have to wait for in the morning is the griddle to get hot enough. Wait until a drop of water flicked on the griddle skitters all over the surface before evaporating, and then it is time to pour on the batter.

Usually, a pancake is ready to flip when little bubbles form at the top, then pop, but it can't hurt to peek under the edge as well.

Please don't smash down pancakes with a spatula to hasten their cooking. It annoys the pancake, does not improve the final product, and only saves you a few seconds anyway.

Serve these pancakes on a warm plate with all the usual good stuff such as butter and warm maple syrup. They are particularly good with Fried Bananas (see page 27).

NO WAFFLES YET, BUT SIN IS COMING

My basic waffles must remain a secret for the time being. I'm aware that somewhere between four and 8,172 people rushed out to buy my first book in hopes of learning that recipe, and it's *still* not here. The reason, simply, is that we're still planning to market our own mix one day, and people will just have to wait.

On the other hand, I've lost my feelings of protectiveness about our Chocolate Sin dessert, so you can look for that in my third book, coming some decade soon to a bookstore near you.

¾ cup buttermilk	1 Tbsp. sugar
½ cup toasted oats (see page 19)	3 Tbsp. oat bran
1 package dry yeast (check the expiration date!)	3 Tbsp. toasted wheat germ
	2 Tbsp. nonfat dry milk powder
¼ cup warm water (about 110°)	½ cup cornmeal
2 eggs	¾ cup whole wheat flour
¼ cup dark molasses	¼ tsp. baking soda, sifted
½ tsp. salt	

In a small bowl, combine the buttermilk and oats and let soak for 20 minutes. Dissolve the yeast in warm water and stir. Set aside for 5 minutes. In a large bowl, mix together the rest of ingredients except the baking soda. Add the buttermilk-soaked oats, the soda, and the yeast mixture, combine, and let the batter sit for 30 minutes. Stir and pour pancake batter onto the griddle. Tiny bubbles will form. When they pop, flip the pancakes over and brown on the other side.

One of the most extraor-
dinary letters I've ever re-
ceived came from a
woman, a recovering alco-
holic, telling me about
the experience she'd had
on the back deck of the
restaurant. It was a beautiful day in spring, replete
with flowers and
hummingbirds. She had a
transcendent experience,
an epiphany, right there
on my deck, about how
she wanted her life to be.
She said that she wanted
to be in her life the way
Cafe Beaujolais is in *its*
life, doing what it does so
well and in such a coordi-
nated manner. I like to
think that Cafe Beaujolais
has such a personal feel-
ing because I am very in-
volved in it on a daily
basis.

COTTAGE CHEESE PANCAKES

Makes 8 or 9 pancakes

Chris is delighted that the preparations for this book have forced me to test pancake recipes at home. He loves pancakes and can't get enough of them. Our old-fashioned stove has a griddle right on the top, for which I am extremely grateful. When I was growing up, "pancake Sundays" were big productions because the waffle and pancake griddles were kept in the back of a deep cupboard and had to be excavated.

When I was older, I lived with a family as an *au pair* helper and was impressed that the mother kept pancake batter in her refrigerator at all times. She made pancakes for her children *even on school days*. That seemed very exciting to me. This recipe is my attempt to recreate her fabulous pancakes. Unlike most, they do *not* have the characteristic bubbles that pop on schedule, announcing that the pancakes are done on the first side and ready to be flipped. You'll have to lift up the edge and peer under to see when they are golden brown and ready for flipping.

3 eggs
1 cup small-curd cottage cheese
2 Tbsp. vegetable oil
1/4 cup white flour

1/4 tsp. baking powder
1/4 tsp. salt
3/4 cup berries that have been frozen (optional)

Place all the ingredients, except the berries, in a blender and combine on low speed. The mixture should be smooth. Pour the batter onto a lightly greased, hot griddle, in 3-inch circles. Place the optional frozen berries on the batter. When both sides are golden brown, serve on warm plate with warm berry syrup.

DECK →

OMA LEAH'S POTATO PANCAKES

Makes about 9 pancakes

Oma Leah was my friend Hilde Burton's grandmother, and Hilde passed the recipe along to me when she learned that I was looking for a really good potato pancake. I have fond memories of some wonderful breakfasts at the Burton household.

Since most of the fun of eating potato pancakes is eating the crispy crunchy part, the trick here is to make them so thin that virtually all the parts are crispy and crunchy.

These are so good, they find their way onto my table at other times of the day as well, in places where a starch is appropriate. I especially like them with an entrée that has lots of sauce, such as a chicken stew.

2 large Idaho potatoes (also known as russets)	¼ tsp. ground ginger
2 Tbsp. grated yellow onion	¼ tsp. salt
1 tsp. white flour	¼ tsp. black pepper
	About ⅓ cup vegetable oil

Peel, then coarsely grate the potatoes to make elongated, very thin strips. Mix with the grated onion. Combine the rest of the ingredients, except oil, and add to potatoes.

Heat some of the oil in a heavy-bottomed skillet (mine is of cast iron and 12 inches across) and, when very hot but not smoking, drop three blobs of mixture into the pan and flatten them out. The pancakes should be about 4 inches in diameter and thin. If they are too thick, they won't get crisp enough.

Reduce the heat and cook for about 3 minutes. Check to see that the underside is richly browned before flipping, then cook for another 3 minutes on the other side. Continue with the rest of the potato mixture, adding more oil as needed.

Serve with sour cream and applesauce.

The restaurant is the
same size that it was five
years ago. A deck in the
garden takes care of over-
flow seating in very nice
weather. But I really like it
small. I still agree with
everything I've ever said
before about the effect
that a change in the size
would have on the feel of
the place; it would just
be inappropriate.
    Growth has come in
the form of our brick
oven that we now use for
bread as well as pizzas
and in the expansion of
the Cafe Beaujolais
Bakery mail-order busi-
ness.

PUMPKIN AND GINGER PANCAKES

Makes 10 to 12 pancakes

I find myself longing for pumpkin at times of the year other than Thanksgiving. For years, that seemed somehow to be strictly forbidden. But I can eat a pumpkin pie at any hour of the day, on any day of the week, and now I feel the same way about these pancakes. I had breakfast with my friend Anne Wertheim once. She whipped these up, and I fell completely in love with them. Anne is not easy to describe. She is an art consultant, the author of a book on tidepools for the Sierra Club, *and* she knows what to do with pumpkins all year long.

There are very few processed ingredients that I will use with absolutely no qualms, but canned pumpkin is right up there as number one. It's just pure pumpkin, with no adulterants. The pancakes are friendly and hearty and unusually good when served with Gingered Butter (recipe follows).

1 cup white flour	½ tsp. powdered ginger
¼ tsp. salt	1 egg, beaten
2 Tbsp. brown sugar	½ cup plain yogurt
1 tsp. baking powder	¾ cup milk
½ tsp. baking soda	¾ cup canned pumpkin
½ tsp. cinnamon	2 Tbsp. melted butter
½ tsp. nutmeg	

In a medium-sized bowl, sift together the flour, salt, brown sugar, baking powder, baking soda, cinnamon, nutmeg, and powdered ginger. In a separate bowl, combine the remaining ingredients. Add the flour mixture and stir until just blended.

Heat a pancake griddle until a drop of water flicked on the surface skates about. Grease the surface, then use about ¼ cup batter per pancake. When the bubbles on the surface of the pancake pop, flip it over to cook on the other side until browned. Serve with Gingered Butter and warm maple syrup.

GINGERED BUTTER

2 Tbsp. finely chopped candied ginger	¼ cup softened butter

Beat the ginger and butter together.

CRANBERRY AND BLUEBERRY PANCAKES

Makes about 18 pancakes

MENDOCINO: OUR ONLY LOCATION

A few years ago, I seriously considered the idea of opening one or more branches. But when push came to shove, I knew I it wouldn't work. Either I would be spending all my time in the car, going from place to place, or I would relinquish full control to someone else at the other location and I felt comfortable with neither alternative.

Actually this recipe could be made with just blueberries—or, on July 4 (July 14 in France), you could use both blueberries and cranberries, and end up with a red, white, and blue (well, red, pancake, and blue) breakfast. I wouldn't use the cranberries alone; they are a little too tart.

When berries are added to a batter, they bleed and the batter takes on a distinctly unappetizing grayish cast. For this reason, we freeze the berries before adding them.

How long do frozen berries last? Well, in my parents' freezer, in the spring of 1989, I found a package that had been frozen in 1981. I used them in these pancakes, and they worked perfectly. Incidentally, my dad is in seventh heaven as we test various pancake recipes morning, noon, and night.

1½ cups white flour
1½ Tbsp. sugar
1½ tsp. salt
1½ tsp. baking powder
1 tsp. baking soda
2 eggs, separated

2 cups buttermilk
¼ cup butter, melted and cooled
2 cups berries that have been frozen

Sift the dry ingredients into bowl. In a separate bowl, mix together the egg yolks, buttermilk, and butter. Add the flour mixture to the eggs and blend. Beat the egg whites until stiff, but not dry, and fold into the batter. Make pancakes on a properly heated griddle (water sprinkled on it will skate around in little balls). Sprinkle berries on top. Flip and cook until golden brown. Serve on heated plates with warm syrup.

HEIDI'S BAKED SUNDAY PANCAKE

Serves 4

Oven-baked pancakes come in many forms, all of them cooked in the oven rather than on the griddle. This one is distinctive because of its custardy consistency. It's really closer to Yorkshire pudding than to flapjacks. You can dress it up with fresh fruit (berries in season are fantastic) or leave it plain and serve it with jam. It is both delicious and attractive on your table.

Heidi Cusick lives with her family just north of Cafe Beaujolais. She teaches cooking in the Mendocino area and writes a weekly cooking column for our local paper, the *Beacon,* and frequent articles on food for the *San Francisco Chronicle.* They keep two sheep, right here in downtown Mendocino. They are not exactly quiet creatures (the sheep, that is, not the Cusicks), and the bleating carries, with remarkable clarity, into my office at the restaurant. It occurs to me that they probably don't have this problem at Lutèce or "21."

3 Tbsp. butter, melted	½ cup white flour
3 eggs	½ tsp. vanilla extract
¾ cup milk	Pinch salt
1½ Tbsp. sugar	

Preheat the oven to 475°. Brush butter on the bottom and sides of a 10-inch cast-iron frying pan with an ovenproof handle. Set the pan in the freezer while you make the batter. In a mixing bowl, beat the eggs until light and lemon colored. Add the remaining ingredients and beat until smooth. Remove the pan from freezer and pour in the batter. Bake at 475° for 5 minutes, then lower the temperature to 400°. Bake for 10 minutes, then lower the temperature to 350° and bake for 10 minutes more. The pancake will be puffed and slightly browned. Run a spatula around the pancake and slide it out onto a serving platter. Sprinkle with powdered sugar and serve at once.

LIGHT-AS-A-FEATHER WHOLE WHEAT AND WILD RICE WAFFLES

Makes about 8 waffles

Whole wheat flour has developed a reputation for producing foods that are heavy, but this doesn't have to be the case. These waffles, for example, are light because the eggs are separated and the whites folded in.

If you have ever tried the commercially available frozen waffles, I'm sure you agree with me that they are, by and large, just awful. And there is no reason to use those horrors when you can keep a large store of your own in the freezer for hurried times. Simply make these waffles ahead of time, cool, then wrap them in foil and freeze. When you're ready to eat them, place them, unwrapped, directly on the rack of a preheated 350° oven, and you'll have them ready to eat almost at once.

If you don't have or don't want to use wild rice, you can use toasted nuts or even tame brown rice, although it doesn't have the nice nutty flavor of the wild. (One of our popular breakfast entrées is a Wild and Crazy Waffle prepared with a sprinkling of both wild rice and toasted pecans.)

2 cups whole wheat flour	4 eggs, separated
2½ tsp. baking powder	1 cup yogurt
¾ tsp. baking soda	1⅓ cups milk
½ tsp. salt	⅓ cup melted butter or corn oil
2 Tbsp. honey	1½ cups cooked wild rice

In a large bowl, sift together the flour, baking powder and soda, and salt. In a separate bowl, blend together the honey, egg yolks, yogurt, milk, and oil or butter. Add the dry mixture to the wet, blending thoroughly. Beat the egg whites until stiff but not dry and fold them into batter. Make waffles according to the directions on your waffle iron, sprinkling about 3 Tbsp. wild rice over the batter for each waffle after it has been poured onto the waffle iron.

SAP

Sometimes I wonder how
it came about that
people eat so many
sweet things in the morn-
ing. Consider maple
syrup. Who was the first
person to say, "This pan-
cake needs something.
How about the sap of
that tree over there?"

TROPICAL WAFFLES WITH MACADAMIA NUTS AND TOASTED COCONUT

Makes about 8 waffles

Our customers always seem to like all the different ways in which we experiment with waffles. Macadamia nuts, expensive and luxurious, happened to be in great supply once at the restaurant, and that inspired me to create this recipe. This seemed to be a nice variation on the theme. Coconut is always popular in the restaurant, no matter how we serve it. Even though I don't think of myself as a big fan of coconut, every time it comes along, I am surprised, all over again, by how much I like it.

2 cups white flour
2½ tsp. baking powder
¾ tsp. baking soda
½ tsp. salt
1 Tbsp. + 1½ tsp. sugar
4 eggs, separated
1 cup yogurt
1½ cups milk

¾ cup + 2 Tbsp. unsalted butter, melted, or corn oil, or a combination of the two
¾ cup chopped toasted macadamia nuts
½ cup toasted, sweetened flaked coconut
Optional toppings: bananas, pineapple chunks, and maple syrup

Sift together the flour, baking powder, baking soda, salt, and sugar. In a separate bowl, beat together the egg yolks, yogurt, milk, and melted butter. Add to the dry ingredients and mix together thoroughly.

Beat the egg whites until stiff but not dry and fold them in along with the nuts and coconut. Make waffles according to the directions on the waffle iron.

These are delicious served with sliced bananas, fresh or canned pineapple chunks, *and* maple syrup.

TROU PAIN PERDU

My dear friend Robert Reynolds has a small restaurant in San Francisco, Le Trou Robert. His charming style and creative culinary offerings have delighted me on many occasions, including our wedding reception.

Robert offers this recipe for French toast that he first tasted in a little house on the shores of Lake Memphremagog, Vermont, prepared with local milk, butter, and garden-fresh fruit. Happily, he has modified the recipe just enough so that I feel no obligation to call it Memphremagog Toast, although you may do so if you feel a particular affinity for the Memphremagog region. (Note: This may be the only recipe in history to mention Memphremagog three, no four, times.)

1 baguette sliced into 1-inch slices	¼ cup sugar
1½ cups milk	Pinch salt
4 eggs	1 Tbsp. vanilla extract
¼ cup orange juice	2 Tbsp. Grand Marnier (optional)
	Butter for sautéing

Set the slices of baguette into a 9- by 13-inch pan. Whisk together all the other ingredients until blended and pour over the bread, turning the slices to coat them thoroughly. Cover the pan with plastic wrap and refrigerate for at least 1 hour.

Heat the butter in a large skillet. After it foams but before it browns, add the bread, turning when golden brown. If you like your French toast custardy, serve it now. If you prefer it a little drier, continue to cook longer. Serve with warmed maple syrup and fresh fruit.

IF ICE CREAM DIDN'T EXIST

If ice cream didn't exist and someone came along and said, "I've found a fantastic new way to combine my favorite breakfast ingredients: cream, sugar, and fruit and then, remarkably, I freeze it!" we'd all be eating ice cream for breakfast and thinking nothing of it.

BANANA, PECAN, AND PINEAPPLE ICE CREAM WAFFLE SUNDAE

Makes about 9 waffles

Several years ago *Food and Wine* magazine interviewed me for an article on home cooking and asked for a new recipe. One morning, lying in bed thinking, "What am I going to concoct?" I found this recipe floating into my mind. Was it creativity or early morning hunger that inspired me?

The name of it may be the wildest part, especially for those people who don't usually eat ice cream in the morning. But we all eat sweet things and we eat creamy things and we eat cold things, so what's wrong with a sweet cold creamy thing such as ice cream, especially in a dish like this? It's just a nice fun dish. I do it with fresh pineapple, but you could use the canned pineapple that comes in its own juice, not heavy syrup.

2 cups white flour, unsifted	1 cup sour cream
1 tsp. cinnamon	1½ cups milk
¼ tsp. nutmeg	¾ cup + 2 Tbsp. butter, or unflavored vegetable oil, or a combination of the two
2½ tsp. baking powder	
¾ tsp. baking soda	
½ tsp. salt	1½ cups mashed ripe bananas
1 Tbsp. + 1½ tsp. sugar	1½ cups chopped toasted pecans
4 eggs, separated	

To make the waffles: Sift together the flour, cinnamon, nutmeg, baking powder, baking soda, salt, and sugar. Set aside. In a separate bowl, beat together the egg yolks, sour cream, milk, butter and/or oil, and bananas. Add the pecans and stir them in along with the dry ingredients. Mix together until well blended. Beat the egg whites until stiff but not dry and fold them into the banana mixture. Bake according to the waffle iron manufacturer's directions.

Serve the waffle on a warmed plate with a scoop of vanilla ice cream topped with the Chunky Pineapple Sauce (recipe follows).

CHUNKY PINEAPPLE SAUCE

3½ cups pineapple chunks
¾ cup Simple Syrup (see recipe below)
1¼ cups hand-chopped pineapple

2 Tbsp. + 1 tsp. lemon juice (more or less, depending on the sweetness of the pineapple)

To make the pineapple sauce: Place the pineapple chunks in the bowl of a food processor fitted with the S-blade, and turn it into purée. Mix together the purée, half a cup of the Simple Syrup, and 2 Tbsp. of the lemon juice. Taste to determine if more syrup and/or lemon juice are needed. Stir in the hand-chopped pineapple and warm gently.

SIMPLE SYRUP
3 cups sugar

1½ cups water

Stir the sugar and water together in a small saucepan over medium heat until the sugar is dissolved. Turn the heat to high and bring to a boil. Boil uncovered and *without stirring* for 5 minutes. Let cool. (This will last for a very long time in the refrigerator.)

I'm fascinated by the idea of a temporary restaurant relocation. Paul Prudhomme took his K-Paul's Restaurant from New Orleans to San Francisco for a month, and the crowds lined up. Barbara Tropp used to bring her Chinese "road show" to Cafe Beaujolais each year. Last year, I had the opportunity to take a bit of Cafe Beaujolais to Barbara's China Moon Cafe in San Francisco for a fund-raising dinner on behalf of Ocean Sanctuary. It was a tremendous amount of work. My planning documents for the trip were not unlike those for the invasion of Normandy.

Right before the event began, the waffle iron gave out, and I envisioned the entire fund raiser crumbling: we lost the Pacific Ocean because Margaret Fox's waffle iron failed. I was wondering if I dialed 9-1-1, could they supply a waffle iron? But at the last minute, it started working, and all was well. The event turned out to be a lot of fun. I wouldn't want to do that every week, but once in a while . . . well, make me an offer.

FRENCH TOASTS

Serves 4 to 6

Following the Mendocino Manual of Style, we offer Apples Butter (see page 67) and now French Toasts. Can Potatoes Pancake be far behind?

My friend Naomi Schwartz owns The Food Company in Gualala, an hour's drive down the coast from Mendocino, where she offers her splendid cooking, both on the premises and in her substantial take-out business.

Naomi's toasts are offered in both a savory version, stuffed with goat or cream cheese, and a sweet version, using ricotta and apples. Both of them are quite rich, so I would serve them with a green or fruit salad. It is a little tricky to slice the bread properly and create the pocket.

Stuffing, either savory or sweet (see below)
1 loaf (1 lb.) good quality bread, preferably homemade, one or two days old
6 eggs

1¼ cups milk
½ tsp. nutmeg
⅛ tsp. salt
1 tsp. vanilla extract (sweet version only)

Make the stuffing mixture first (see below).

Preheat the oven to 375°. Cut the bread at an angle, making the slices almost 2 inches thick. Cut each slice in half diagonally. With a small sharp knife, cut a pocket into each half leaving the crusts intact.

Stuff each triangle with about 2 Tbsp. of stuffing mixture or as much as can be stuffed in without tearing the bread. Beat together the eggs, milk, nutmeg, salt, and vanilla (if used). Immerse the triangles in the liquid for about 5 minutes. It takes quite a long time for the liquid to soak into the bread thoroughly. Melt the butter in a large skillet and when hot, add as many slices as will easily fit. Sauté on both sides until richly browned, then place in the oven for 5 minutes. Garnish with hot mushrooms or apples and serve.

STUFFING FOR SAVORY VERSION

1 lb. goat or cream cheese or a combination of the two
3 Tbsp. minced chives
2 tsp. fresh minced thyme or 1 tsp. dried thyme

2 tsp. fresh minced dill or 1 tsp. dried dill
Salt and freshly ground black pepper
2 lb. mushrooms, sliced
3 Tbsp. unsalted butter

Mix together all the ingredients except the mushrooms and butter. Sauté mushrooms in butter until cooked through but not reduced. Add salt and pepper to taste and set aside for garnish.

90 MORNING FOOD

STUFFING FOR SWEET VERSION

1 lb. ricotta cheese
1½ tsp. freshly grated orange
   zest
1 tsp. vanilla extract
1 tsp. almond extract
⅛ tsp. grated nutmeg

4 medium apples, peeled and
   thinly sliced
3 Tbsp. unsalted butter
½ tsp. cinnamon
2 Tbsp. brown sugar

Mix together the cheese, orange zest, vanilla and almond extracts, and nutmeg. Sauté the apples in butter until softened and cooked all the way through, but not mushy. Add the cinnamon and sugar and cook over low heat for another minute or two, until sugar coats the apple slices evenly. Set aside for garnish.

EGGS

SUMMERTIME OMELETTE
For 1 omelette

You can make this omelette, as I do, from whatever happens to be in the vegetable section of your refrigerator: carrots, spinach, zucchini, mushrooms, bell peppers, green onions, etc. It is hard to imagine any vegetable that wouldn't work.

Some people may think this is a lot of ingredients to combine with only two eggs, but the quantities are fairly small and the volume is reduced by sautéing.

FILLING
- 2 tsp. olive or corn oil or unsalted butter
- ½ cup or a bit more thinly sliced fresh vegetables (see suggestions above)
- Salt and pepper
- 2 cherry tomatoes, cut in half

OMELETTE
- 2 eggs
- 1 tsp. cold water
- 3 drops Tabasco sauce
- 2 tsp. unsalted butter or 1 tsp. butter and 1 tsp. corn oil
- 1 tsp. finely chopped fresh herbs: your choice of tarragon, basil, oregano, chervil, dill, or cilantro
- 1 oz. grated cheese (I enjoy a medium-sharp Cheddar)

Place an 8-inch nonstick pan over medium heat, add the oil or butter and, when warm, add the ½ cup vegetables, tossing with a wooden spatula until they are tender but not limp. Spinach should be added only in the last 20 seconds. Season with salt and pepper and set aside.

Wipe out the pan. With a fork, beat together the eggs, water, and Tabasco sauce until blended. Again, heat the pan over medium heat, add the butter or oil, then the herbs, and immediately pour in the beaten eggs. Let sit on heat for 5 seconds, then grab the pan handle and start to swirl the egg mixture in the pan slowly, paying attention to distributing the herbs evenly.

With a wooden spatula, pull the outside of the eggs toward the center, tilting the pan to allow the uncooked egg to spill into the pan. When the eggs have set, you can flip them if you're feeling adventuresome, or not if you're not. (This depends on how softly cooked you like your eggs.)

To fill, distribute the cheese quickly in a line down the center of the omelette and follow with the cooked vegetables and the tomatoes.

Slowly slide the omelette onto a heated plate until about half is on the plate and half is still in the pan. Then, using the pan to help, fold the other half of the omelette over the top of the half that is already on the plate.

FLIPPING OMELETTES

The only "secret" to omelette making is flipping them. Many times, when I've been teaching a class and I say, "Now you just flip the omelette," people gasp and say, "Oh, I could never do that." But it is really so simple. You jiggle the pan in the right way, and a certain arc is created.

It's just a matter of practice, but a lot of people seem reluctant to practice, because they think of it as a waste of ingredients. But consider this. If you decide to take half an hour to learn to do this (and that is all it should take) you can buy three dozen eggs. That will give you eighteen two-egg omelettes to practice with. Even if you have a succession of small disasters (for which your dog will love you!), you'll get there, for a total investment of less than three dollars, which is considerably less than the price of a cooking class.

So make the three-dollar investment, wait until no one is around to snicker, spread plastic on the floor if necessary, and go for it. It's like learning to swim or ride a bike. Somewhere between the third and twelfth try, suddenly you'll be doing it.

HINGED PANS?

People have asked me about those high-tech omelette pans that are round and hinged in the middle; you put some ingredients in each half and then fold up the pan as it cooks. I tend to like my eggs a bit less done, and that method encourages cooking them extra firm.

BLUE CHEESE, BACON, APPLE, AND WALNUT OMELETTE

Makes 1 omelette

I like to combine eggs with cheese and fruit, and it occurred to me that this would be an interesting and pleasant combination of both flavors and textures. The saltiness and smokiness of the bacon goes well with the tanginess of the blue cheese. Under other circumstances, the apple would be too much, but here it comes between blue cheese and the bacon, to prevent any competition of flavors.

It could be argued that the eggs are almost incidental to this omelette; they just lend credence to the filling, while holding the whole works together.

In making omelettes, I always try to put the cheese in first, right on the egg, to give it a chance to melt completely, or at least to soften. I especially like the Maytag brand of blue cheese, which comes from the same Iowa family that brings us those appliances, but any good blue cheese will do.

This omelette has nearly enough ingredients for a complete breakfast. I would serve it with a muffin or with some potatoes.

FILLING
1 oz. blue cheese
1 Tbsp. sour cream
2 Tbsp. toasted walnuts, coarsely
    chopped and bounced
    around in a sieve for about 30
    seconds to remove as much
    of the skin as possible; the
    walnut hair or fuzz or
    whatever it's called sticks to
    the sieve, leaving you with
    naked little walnuts
1/6 to 1/4 of a green apple, thinly
    sliced (depends on the size
    of apple)
4 tsp. butter
2 Tbsp. cooked crumbled bacon

OMELETTE
2 eggs
2 tsp. cold water
2 drops Tabasco sauce

Mix the blue cheese, sour cream, and walnuts and set aside. Sauté the apple slices in 2 tsp. of the butter just until soft (about 3 minutes) and set aside. Have the crumbled bacon handy.

Beat the eggs together with the water and Tabasco sauce until the yolks and whites are blended. Do not overbeat. Heat an 8-inch pan (I use Silverstone™ exclusively, because it never sticks) until it is quite hot and add the remaining 2 tsp. butter. It should sizzle. In the next few seconds, pour the eggs into the pan.

Start rotating the pan over the flame in order to form a cohesive mass. You can help this along by pushing the outside of the eggs toward the center with a wooden spatula. The second the eggs are no longer liquid, layer in the filling down the center: first the blue cheese mixture, then the sautéed apples, and then the crumbled bacon. Fold and serve immediately on a warmed plate.

At Cafe Beaujolais, I flip the eggs so the top becomes the bottom and then add the filling. It depends on how creamy you prefer your eggs; they are creamier when cooked only on one side.

IS IT ALL RIGHT TO EAT EGGS AND BUTTER?

Eggs have an increasingly evil image. At the restaurant, we hear more and more people lamenting the fact that eggs aren't good for them anymore (as if they ever were) . . . but then they proceed to eat everything we put in front of them. I haven't noticed any lessening in egg orders, although from time to time, someone will order an omelette or scrambled eggs made with whites only, or one yolk with three whites.

They keep coming out with all these healthier substitutes for eggs and for butter and so forth, but the point is that none of them tastes as good as the real thing and some are utterly unacceptable. I choose simply to eat less of the real thing. I think more people should plan ahead, if only for two or three meals. Forethought on the lines of: "I will eat egg yolks for breakfast, but I won't butter my bread at lunch or dinner." That sort of thing.

ANDOUILLE OMELETTE FILLING

Enough for 4 omelettes

DO WHAT YOU WILL
BUT DON'T LEAVE OUT
THE GARLIC

Let these recipes be guidelines or suggestions, not limitations for omelette making. Always feel free to substitute one thing for another, with the possible exception of garlic. If you don't use the garlic, I may have to confiscate your book.

We rarely go out and buy something just for a particular omelette. Sometimes it seems as if the main reason for having a breakfast restaurant is to get rid of leftovers. Not every ingredient starts out being a leftover, of course, but if someone doesn't use it quickly, it will be. For this reason, I had quite a difficult time writing down these seemingly simple recipes. Usually I go into the walk-in refrigerator and select whatever strikes my fancy. Even if you can't walk into your refrigerator, the philosophy is the same.

For quite a while, this was our best-selling omelette in the restaurant on Sundays; people go wild for it. We could make it by the cement-truck-full.

1 eggplant (slightly less than 1 lb.)	1 tsp. garlic, minced
2 tsp. salt	Salt and freshly ground black pepper
1 medium zucchini	⅓ cup Herbed Cream Cheese (see page 132)
8 oz. spicy sausage (we use andouille links)	1 tomato, chopped
3 Tbsp. olive oil	3 Tbsp. toasted pine nuts

Dice the eggplant into ½-inch cubes; should make about 2 cups. Sprinkle the eggplant with 2 tsp. salt and place in a colander. Let it drain for 30 minutes, then press down on the cubes to remove as much more liquid as possible.

Cut the zucchini into half circles by slicing it once lengthwise, then crosswise into thin slices. Bake or poach the sausage and cool.

Pat the eggplant dry and sauté in olive oil over medium heat until it is extremely soft. When nearly done, add the zucchini and garlic and continue cooking for another 3 minutes. Season with salt and pepper and set aside to cool.

Slice the sausage and fry until brown. Mix together all the ingredients and taste for seasoning. Heat for 5 minutes in a 375° oven before filling the omelettes.

BACON AND GOAT CHEESE OMELETTE FILLING

Enough for 4 omelettes

We usually use a combination of greens, depending on what the local farmers have brought in that day. And we use Laura Chenel's California Chèvre; it's just goaty enough to be interesting but not overwhelming.

6 strips (8 if skinny) uncooked bacon, diced

1 cup finely chopped leeks or green onions

3 Tbsp. olive oil

1 tsp. minced garlic

5 cups spinach, chard, bok choy, beet greens, kale, or any other green that can be cooked, cut into ribbons (stack the leaves and cut into strips 3/4-inch wide; use the stems if they are tender)

Salt and freshly ground pepper

8 oz. goat cheese

2 Tbsp. sour cream

Fry the bacon until done and drain. Sauté the leeks or onions in olive oil until just tender. Add the garlic to the pan and then the greens and sauté over medium heat until tender and reduced. (Greens deflate dramatically, by as much as 75 percent.) Remove from heat and season with salt and pepper. Crumble the goat cheese and mix in. If the mixture seems dry, add sour cream. Heat the filling for 5 minutes in a 375° oven before using in omelettes.

FETA CHEESE AND RISO OMELETTE FILLING

Enough for 4 omelettes

Riso (which means rice) is actually a tiny rice-shaped pasta. This is, thus, a sneaky way of introducing the idea of pasta in the morning. Next thing you know, someone will leave out the omelette part entirely and serve this heated in a bowl.

¼ lb. riso pasta
⅓ lb. feta cheese, crumbled
½ cup finely chopped green onions
1 ripe tomato, seeded and chopped

¼ cup brined (Greek) olives, pitted and coarsely chopped
3 Tbsp. finely chopped fresh basil
3 Tbsp. pine nuts
Freshly ground black pepper

In boiling salted water, cook the pasta until tender (about 8 to 10 minutes). Drain, run cold water over the pasta, then drain again. When cool, combine all the ingredients. Heat in a 375° oven for about 5 minutes before filling the omelettes.

CHICKEN LIVER OMELETTE FILLING

Enough for 4 omelettes

When I first came to Mendocino in 1975 and ate at Cafe Beaujolais (having little notion that one day I would own it!), I often ordered the Pitsenbargers' chicken liver omelette, which was very good, and one of the few things I could then afford.

I challenged Chris to come up with a chicken liver recipe that I would enjoy at least as much, and the result surpassed my already high expectations. I love the flavor that the fresh herbs impart. That's what makes the dish truly special, in my opinion.

Some people are not filled with enthusiasm about performing surgery on the chicken livers, but it is essential in order to prevent bitterness and an odd texture, so grit your teeth and do it. No big deal, and the result is well worth it.

2 medium yellow onions (about 1½ lb.), chopped
6 Tbsp. butter
2 tsp. salt
2 tsp. fresh sage or marjoram, chopped

6 chicken livers (about 12 oz., the palest available)
Freshly ground pepper
⅓ cup port, sherry, or Madeira

Sauté the onions in butter with a big pinch of salt over very low heat for about 25 minutes, until golden brown and cooked all the way through. Drain and set the onions aside in a bowl, keeping the butter. Add the herb of your choice to the onions and stir.

Wash the livers and remove membranes and any green spots. Pat them dry and season both sides with the remaining salt and some pepper. Pour the butter back into pan, turn the heat to high, and sauté the livers for about 1½ minutes on each side to brown evenly. With a slotted spoon, remove the livers from the pan and add them to the onions. Pour off the fat from the pan, place the pan over high heat and, within a few seconds, add the port. Cook to reduce, scraping the bottom of the pan until only 1 or 2 syrupy tablespoons are left. Pour over the liver and onion mixture and gently combine.

UNSALTED BUTTER

We always use unsalted butter in the restaurant. I like the flavor. Salt is put into butter not just for flavoring, but as a preservative, and it enables the butter to get older without the age being quite so noticeable. I prefer to use fresher ingredients whenever possible and unsalted butter is always fresher.

CHERRY OMELETTE

Serves 1

Many years ago, soon after I took over the restaurant, a Swiss man passing through town paused in his trip to work at Cafe Beaujolais for a few months. One day, he happened to mention that cherry omelettes were quite popular in Switzerland. I must have filed that information away in some deep recess of my brain, but it came back to me recently, perhaps because morning food is on my mind, and cherries had just come into season.

I decided to add the sugar and vanilla, to make it unlike any ordinary omelette, more like a breakfast dessert, and I happen to think it is exceptionally delicious. It's not so sweet that it is really peculiar; just unusual. I would serve it with muffins or toast. My only warning is to exercise care when pitting and chopping cherries to keep the juice from getting under your fingernails. I lived with this recipe for a week and a half, despite frequent scrubbings.

The recipe does work with other fruits, especially berries, but it doesn't have the same texture or quality that cherries bring to it.

FILLING	OMELETTE
½ cup pitted fresh cherries, coarsely chopped	2 eggs
1 Tbsp. sour cream	2 tsp. sugar
	⅛ tsp. vanilla extract
	1 tsp. butter

Beat together the eggs, sugar, and vanilla. In a small nonstick pan, heat the cherries quickly until warm. In another nonstick pan heat the butter until it foams, then add the eggs and make an omelette. When the eggs are set, add the sour cream and then the warm cherries. Fold and serve.

JOANA'S FRITTATA

Serves 2 or 3

Joana Bryar-Matons is a marvelous cook who appears in the first Cafe Beaujolais book with her Catalan Baked Fish, which turned out to be one of the most popular recipes in the whole book. She grew up in Barcelona, where one develops a special appreciation for the things you can do with vegetables, eggs, and olive oil.

This is a wonderful alternative when you don't want just the same old scrambled eggs or omelette. You can be as flexible or creative as you wish with regard to the vegetables. You could add cooked broccoli; you could leave out the mushrooms.

1 tsp. olive oil	Salt and pepper to taste
¼ cup green onion, finely chopped	½ tsp. fresh basil, marjoram, or oregano
¼ cup sliced mushrooms	1 Tbsp. minced fresh parsley
¼ cup bell peppers, diced (a combination of red, green, and yellow looks especially nice)	4 eggs, beaten with ¼ tsp. Tabasco sauce
	1 cup grated cheese
¼ cup peeled and seeded tomatoes	1 Tbsp. grated dry cheese

Heat the olive oil in a 10-inch nonstick pan and add the onion, mushrooms, bell peppers, and tomatoes. Over medium-high heat, sauté until the vegetables have softened slightly (about 1 minute). Season with salt and pepper and add the fresh herb and parsley.

Pour the eggs over the vegetables and sprinkle the cheeses over the surface. Cover with a tight-fitting lid and reduce the heat to the lowest possible. Cook for about 10 minutes, then serve immediately.

HANDS VERSUS MACHINES

There is a lot of chemistry at work in the kitchen, especially in making bread and candy. Sometimes the changes are very subtle and if you are grinding or swirling away at high speed with a food processor or a big electric beater, you simply may not notice.

In bread making, nothing replaces the touch of hand kneading. You should do it that way *at least once* to know exactly how it feels and looks at all stages. Then you might be better able to see what's happening with your electronic four-stage, computer-controlled, selfcontained bread-o-matic.

NOODLE FRITTATA

Serves 1

While assembling the recipes for this book, it was suggested to me that I should include a section entitled "Around the World with Fried Starch." Can I help it if our clientele has a fondness for all those carbohydrates?

I devised this recipe strictly on the basis of what sounded good to me. Noodles and eggs seemed a slight ethnic tilt on the matzoh and eggs dish in my first book. Imagine my surprise when my mother, browsing through one of her vast collection of cookbooks, discovered an old Italian recipe for *Frittata à la Spaghettini.* You guessed it: noodles and eggs.

I say *noodles* and not *pasta* because there is nothing trendy about this recipe. Pasta is trendy; noodles aren't. To me, the recipe is immensely satisfying, as well as fast and easy and quite flexible, as other optional ingredients are added. It is one of the few egg dishes that I prefer well done and browned on the outside. If you don't, you will need to adjust the timing.

1 Tbsp. olive oil	Fried onions and/or cooked vegetables (optional)
2 oz. medium egg noodles, cooked and drained	2 eggs (or 1 whole egg + 2 egg whites)
Salt and freshly ground black pepper	1 scant Tbsp. grated dry cheese

In an 8-inch nonstick pan, heat the oil and add the noodles. Season with salt and pepper and cook over medium heat until golden brown and crunchy. Add the optional fried onions and/or cooked vegetables. Season the eggs and pour them into the pan, covering the noodles completely. Sprinkle the cheese over the surface of the eggs.

Place a lid on the pan and turn down the heat. Cook for about 30 seconds, then remove the lid and flip, either by nimbly tossing the frittata in the air, or by placing a plate over the pan, turning the whole works upside down, and sliding the *frittata* back into the pan. Cook for 15 seconds and serve.

MERRY CHRISTMAS FRITTATA

Serves 3 to 4

It's "Merry Christmas" because of the red and green peppers. Oddly enough the recipe was developed for *Chocolatier* magazine. The editors wanted a whole bunch of chocolate recipes, of course, but they also wanted something that wasn't sweet and that anyone could make from basic ingredients you can get anywhere.

Frittata is similar to a *quiche* and, like a *quiche*, you can serve it hot or cold or anywhere in between, and at any time of the day. At the restaurant, we serve this hotter in the early morning than we do later in the day. People associate breakfast with hot food. Later on, we serve it at room temperature, when I happen to think it tastes best. It tastes good any way you do it, with the possible exception of frozen on a stick. However, to forestall complaints, I do ask our waitresses to explain to people that we *mean* to serve it at room temperature. Incidentally, *frittata* is perfect for a picnic. It keeps well and can be served right out of the picnic basket.

1 Tbsp. butter
½ cup finely chopped red onions
8 eggs, beaten
¾ cup chopped roasted red peppers
½ cup chopped green chiles
2 Tbsp. grated dry cheese (Parmesan, dry Monterey jack, or Asiago)

½ tsp. salt
2 pinches freshly ground black pepper
½ tsp. dried oregano
8 drops Tabasco sauce
1 Tbsp. olive oil
Sliced avocado and/or sour cream, for garnish

Preheat the oven to 350°.

Melt the butter and sauté the onions for about 5 minutes, until they are translucent, not brown.

In a bowl, mix the onions with the eggs, peppers, *chiles*, cheese, salt, pepper, oregano, and Tabasco.

Use the olive oil to coat a 9-inch pan thoroughly. Pour in the *frittata* mixture and bake for 30 minutes. The top should be slightly brown. Serve at room temperature (or not; see above), garnished with sliced avocado and/or sour cream.

CATALAN OMELETTE CAKE (PASTEL DE TRUITA)

Serves 4 to 6

This is the omelette equivalent of *pousse café*. A remarkable idea—four separate *fritattas* (*fritattae?*) stacked up with tomato and eggplant sauce in between. Actually it's my interpretation of pages of almost-impossible-to-read script that arrived from my Spanish friend, Joana. The two very clear things that can be said about it are:

1. It is incredibly messy to make, and

2. It's worth it.

In Joana's version, the finished cake is "frosted" with mayonnaise, but that sounded so bizarre to me that I didn't even try it, although you are more than welcome to do so if you wish. I choose to cover mine with more of the tomato and eggplant sauce and some fresh herbs.

You may add other ingredients to any or all of the layers: mushrooms, other vegetables, and so forth. Serve it at room temperature and don't even *think* about trying to take it on a picnic.

12 eggs
½ tsp. Tabasco sauce
6 Tbsp. olive oil
1 medium red potato, peeled and cut into matchstick-sized pieces
Salt and pepper
¼ cup grated dry cheese
2 cups spinach, cut into ribbons
1 cup quartered marinated artichoke hearts
1½ cups cooked, salted white beans
1 tsp. minced garlic
2 Tbsp. minced fresh parsley
2 cups Tomato-Eggplant Sauce (see page 138)

Beat the eggs with the Tabasco sauce, and divide into four equal parts.

For the potato omelette layer: In a 10-inch nonstick pan, heat 2 Tbsp. of the oil and add potato sticks when the oil is hot but not smoking. Toss the potatoes until they are soft and slightly brown. Season with salt and pepper. With the pan over medium heat, add 1 portion of eggs and mix the potatoes in quickly so they are evenly distributed. Reduce the heat to very low. Sprinkle with 1 Tbsp. of the cheese and cover with a tight-fitting lid. Cook until the eggs are no longer runny (about 3 minutes). Slide the omelette onto a flat surface and keep warm.

For the spinach omelette layer: Heat 1 Tbsp. oil in the pan and add the spinach, stirring and tossing until it has reduced significantly and is tender (about 45 seconds). Season with salt and pepper. Increase the heat and add 1 portion of eggs, mixing to distribute the spinach evenly. Reduce heat to very low. Sprinkle with 1 Tbsp. cheese and cover with a tight-fitting lid. Cook until the eggs are no longer runny (about 3 minutes). Slide the omelette onto a flat surface and keep warm.

For the artichoke omelette layer: Add the artichoke hearts to the pan and heat. Season with salt and pepper. Add 1 tsp. oil, then 1 portion eggs, then 1 Tbsp. cheese. Cover with a lid and cook until eggs are no longer runny (about 4 or 5 minutes). Slide the omelette out onto a flat surface and keep warm.

For the white bean omelette layer: Heat 2 Tbsp. oil in the pan and add the cooked beans, garlic, and parsley. Over low heat, cook about 3 minutes. Try not to mash the beans. Season with pepper. Add the last portion of eggs and mix gently to distribute evenly. Sprinkle with 1 Tbsp. cheese. Cover with the lid and cook over low heat for 3 minutes. Slide out onto your serving plate, which should be completely flat.

To assemble the cake: Mash the warm Tomato-Eggplant Sauce a little so that no pieces of eggplant will create lumps in your "cake." Measure slightly less than a quarter of the sauce onto the middle of the white bean layer. Spread evenly all the way to the edges. Carefully transfer the artichoke layer onto the top of the sauce. Add more sauce, then the spinach layer, then more sauce, and then the potato layer. Add the remaining sauce, using it to cover the top and sides, as if you were frosting a cake. Sprinkle with parsley and cut into wedges to serve.

BREAKFAST BURRITO

Serves 1

There are times when I think that plain simple scrambled eggs with toast is my very favorite kind of morning food. But even *I* like a change once in a while, and the breakfast *burrito* is a splendid variation.

This may not technically be a *burrito*, since I don't fold either end over; it is simply a tube. And since you will be rolling these up, be sure not to overcook the *tortilla*, or you will be well on your way to creating breakfast *nachos*, which may not be a bad idea, come to think of it.

I eat these with my hands, but I notice that others use a knife and fork. I wouldn't eat this over an Oriental carpet, since the cheese does tend to ooze out the ends a bit, but nothing to worry about. You can make them as plain or as fancy as you wish. Before rolling, you can add one or more additional ingredients of your choice: avocadoes, tomatoes, olives, diced sausage or other meats, and/or sour cream.

2 flour tortillas (7 or 8 inches in diameter)
½ cup (2 oz.) grated Monterey jack, Cheddar, or Swiss cheese
2 eggs
Tabasco sauce

Salt and freshly ground black pepper
1 tsp. butter or oil
2 Tbsp. chopped green onions
2 Tbsp. salsa

In the oven: Preheat the oven to 350°. Place the *tortillas* on a cookie sheet and sprinkle with cheese. Put them in the oven long enough for the cheese to melt and the tortillas to brown lightly in spots (about 4 to 5 minutes).

On the stovetop: Heat a pan large enough to accommodate a *tortilla*. Warm the *tortilla* for about 1 minute. The heated side should begin to brown slightly. Flip and sprinkle cheese evenly over the surface. Cover for about 1 minute, or until the cheese is melted. Keep warm while preparing the second *tortilla* in the same way.

When the *tortillas* are nearly ready, beat the eggs with several drops of Tabasco sauce and salt and pepper as desired. Heat the butter in a separate pan, add green onions, stir for a few seconds, and add the eggs. Over medium heat, scramble the eggs to your taste. Add *salsa* and stir briefly.

Divide the egg mixture between the 2 *tortillas*, distributing the egg along one-third of each *tortilla*. Add additional ingredients if you wish and roll from the side with the egg on it.

If you want to achieve a more proper *burrito*hood, you could fold up an inch or two of the bottom as you roll it up, making a pocket. Eat immediately.

HUEVOS RANCHEROS

Serves 1

I thought about renaming this dish, but *Huevos Rancheros* is what it is, so that is what it is called. This is *my* way of doing it. Instead of frying the eggs, I poach them in the *salsa*, and they come out so delicious. It takes a little longer than frying them, but no big deal. Once in a while, the egg sticks to the bottom of the pan, but you just run a rubber spatula gently under it and it will come loose.

You can't dawdle when you make this recipe or the eggs will end up hard-cooked. Prepare yourself for precision timing, because the whole thing comes together in about three minutes.

I have made this with homemade Salsa (page 140), but I must confess that when I made it with store-bought Pace Picante Sauce, it was really pretty good.

For some reason, corn *tortillas* only seem to come in a small size, so you need two of them, overlapped. Flour *tortillas* sometimes seem large enough to use as a bedspread, and one will be quite sufficient. If you prepare the recipe for more than one person, increase the *salsa* by about ¼ cup per additional serving.

ON TIPPING

Some etiquette books suggest that the percentage of a tip should be smaller in the morning than it might be later in the day: 10 percent instead of 15 percent, or 15 percent instead of 20 percent. I've never quite understood that; the waiting staff has to work just as hard. Generally, at Cafe Beaujolais, however, tip percentages remain about the same regardless of the time of day.

1 cup Salsa (page 140)
2 eggs
2 corn tortillas or 1 large flour tortilla (10 to 12 inches)
¼ to ½ cup grated Monterey jack or Cheddar cheese
About ¾ cup Black Bean Chili (see page 158), heated
About ½ cup shredded crunchy lettuce (optional)
1 Tbsp. chopped black olives
Sour cream
Chopped cilantro

Heat the *salsa* to near boiling in a small frying pan. Break each egg into a separate small bowl and gently add to the *salsa*. Cover the pan and cook for about 3 minutes, occasionally spooning sauce over eggs, and checking to be sure eggs haven't stuck to the bottom of the pan.

Heat the *tortilla(s)* either on a skillet on top of the stove or in a 350° oven. Sprinkle cheese evenly over the surface of the *tortilla(s)* and let it melt. Remove from heat and spread with Chili. If using lettuce, place around the edge of the *tortilla*.

With a large spoon, carefully remove the eggs from the *salsa* and place in middle of your creation. Spoon *salsa* over the top and garnish with olives, sour cream, and cilantro. Serve immediately.

PERSIAN EGGS

Serves 2

This is another recipe from Anni Amberger, although as far as I know, it was never served to Stevie Wonder. It's a baked egg dish with a very nice blend of flavors and it comes out quite differently depending on whether you use curry or saffron. It is one of those egg dishes in which the total appears to be more than the sum of its parts, what with the presentation on a bed of vegetables with interesting textures and flavors. It seems quite intricate, but it is really easy to put together.

When I was testing the recipe, I had a tendency to overbake the eggs, which isn't terrible, but it is better when they have firm whites and runny yolks. So be careful. You may want to try this once or twice before serving it to guests.

You can also use two ovenproof baking dishes instead of the pan if you wish to make individual servings.

2 Tbsp. olive oil
2 tomatoes, peeled and chopped
½ cup finely chopped onion
½ cup finely chopped green pepper
½ cup finely chopped mushrooms
1 tsp. minced garlic
¼ tsp. Beaujolais Blend Herbs (see page xv) or oregano
Either ½ tsp. curry powder or 2 pinches saffron

3 Tbsp. lemon juice
Salt and freshly ground black pepper to taste
4 eggs
2 Tbsp. grated dry cheese (Parmesan, dry Monterey jack, Asiago, etc.)
½ cup grated cheese (Monterey jack, Cheddar, or Swiss)
Chopped parsley or cilantro for topping

Preheat the oven to 350°.

In a large ovenproof frying pan, heat the oil and sauté the tomatoes, onion, pepper, mushrooms, and garlic for 3 minutes. Add the herbs, spice, and lemon juice, salt and pepper to taste, and cook for 1 more minute.

Smooth out the vegetables and make four evenly spaced depressions on the vegetable bed. Carefully crack an egg into each depression and sprinkle with the cheeses. Place the frying pan in the oven for 12 to 15 minutes, until the eggs are just set. Serve immediately, sprinkled with chopped parsley or cilantro.

SPINACH SOUFFLÉ

Serves 6 to 8

"Soufflé" has become a catch-all term at Cafe Beaujolais for dishes that we aren't quite sure how to identify. In this case, it is a marketing decision too. Whether customers order a dish or not frequently depends on the name. For example, pudding and casserole are not winners. Soufflé generally is.

Of course I prefer fresh vegetables most of the time, but this recipe works well with frozen spinach and, by the time it gets all the other ingredients added to it, is quite indistinguishable from the fresh. The soufflé can be eaten hot or cold. It has a solidness about it, but it's not a rock. I would serve this for breakfast or brunch and I've packed it along on picnics. It is quite versatile for a little loaf. And, like so many other recipes, it can be embroidered upon, as you wish, without endangering the quality. Some people may wish to add garlic or pesto, for instance. You might even think about trading in the spinach for broccoli, which would have to be blanched or precooked a bit. Please remember to adjust the name of the recipe according to the vegetable used.

1 cup minced onions

2 Tbsp. butter and/or oil

2 packages (10 oz. each) frozen chopped spinach, defrosted and squeezed as dry as possible.

1 cup grated dry cheese (Asiago, dry Monterey jack, or Parmesan)

½ cup cottage or ricotta cheese

½ cup dry bread crumbs

4 eggs, separated

2 Tbsp. chopped fresh basil, oregano or tarragon, or 1 tsp. Beaujolais Blend Herbs (see page xv)

¼ tsp. ground nutmeg

¾ tsp. salt

¼ tsp. freshly ground pepper

WHITE SAUCE

2 Tbsp. butter

2 Tbsp. white flour

1½ cups warm milk

Preheat the oven to 350°. Sauté the onions in butter or oil for 10 minutes until golden brown. Add the spinach and cook briefly, about 1 minute, to dry out. Transfer to a large bowl, allow to cool, then add the cheeses, bread crumbs, egg yolks, herbs, nutmeg, salt, and pepper, and stir to combine. Set aside.

Make a white sauce as follows. Over medium heat, melt butter in a pan and add the flour, stirring for 3 minutes without browning. Add the warm milk and stir for 5 more minutes. The sauce should be thick and smooth. Cook briefly and add it to spinach mixture. Beat the egg whites until stiff but not dry and fold in. Pour into a buttered 9-inch square pan and bake for 35 minutes. Serve immediately or, if you don't mind a somewhat deflated soufflé, serve later at room temperature.

OLE SOUFFLE

Serves 4 to 6

Notice the absence of accent marks on the name of this recipe. That's because it is pronounced "OH-lee SOOF-ull," who may have been the Norwegian sea captain who first . . . . Would you be more likely to order Pudding Olé? See. It does have egg whites folded in, so the French Soufflé Acceptance Board might at least take our application. But it also has these lovely Latin touches, that make the finished product spicy and delicious.

Ole Souffle can be a side dish served with Black Bean Chili (see page 158), or it can be an entrée all its own, perhaps with fresh fruit or a green salad on the side.

¾ cup creamed corn	1 cup grated sharp Cheddar cheese
2 eggs, separated	2 Tbsp. finely chopped jalapeño chiles
2 Tbsp. corn oil	Sour cream
½ cup + 1 Tbsp. milk	Salsa
¾ cup cornmeal	Chopped green onions
½ tsp. salt	Cilantro
½ tsp. baking soda	

Preheat the oven to 350°. Combine the corn, egg yolks, oil, and milk. In a separate bowl, mix cornmeal, salt, and soda, and add to the liquids, mixing well. Beat the egg whites until stiff but not dry and fold in quickly.

Pour half of this mixture into a greased 8-inch-square pan, sprinkle evenly with the cheese and *chiles.* Pour the remaining batter over, smooth to cover and bake for about 30 minutes. Test for doneness with a knife inserted in the center: If it emerges clean, the soufflé is done. Let cool on a rack about 3 to 5 minutes. It will deflate a little. Cut into 4 to 6 servings and serve with a dollop of sour cream, some *salsa,* chopped green onions, and cilantro.

SALZBURGER NOCKERL

Serves 4

Stephanie Kroninger, a dear friend and an immensely talented graphic artist, retrieved this recipe from her family files. A *nockerl* is a traditional German and Austrian item that is a cross between noodles and dumplings with a touch of popovers and some elements of meringue. We really don't have anything like it in this country, which makes it impossible to describe. But I'm about to try.

You make a soufflé of sorts, although it is not as substantial as most soufflés are; just a fluffy mixture. You ladle little blobs into a pan, cook them ever so slightly, and then stick them in the oven where they rise a bit. They don't hold at all. They start to deflate the moment they are served, so you've got to eat them as soon as they are done. Depending on the idiosyncrasies of your oven, you may want to use the upper rack to ensure browning.

Although I prefer the lesser amount of sugar, I will admit that the greater amount produces a more attractive mound. But there are hardly any redeeming values to these (sorry, Stephanie), other than that they taste pretty darn good and it is fun to say, "Let's have *Salzburger Nockerl* this morning, dear," and two hours later, you still can't get up from the table.

2 Tbsp. clarified butter	⅓ to ½ cup sugar
4 eggs, separated	3 Tbsp. flour
⅛ tsp. cream of tartar	Zest from 1 lemon
⅛ tsp. salt	

Preheat the oven to 325°. Melt the butter in a 10- or 12-inch ovenproof pan. (I use cast iron.) Set aside. Beat the egg whites with the cream of tartar and salt until foamy. Gradually beat in the sugar, 1 tablespoon at a time, beating after each addition until the egg whites are glossy and satiny. Continue beating until the whites form stiff peaks, that is, until the egg whites will stand straight up when the beater is removed from the bowl.

Moving quickly, beat the egg yolks with flour and lemon zest until light in color and thickened. Carefully fold the yolk mixture into the whites. Heat the ovenproof pan and spoon the egg mixture into it, creating 4 mounds. Cook on top of the stove over very low heat until the undersides are golden (about 2 minutes). Place the pan into the oven and bake until the tops are golden (about 7 minutes). Remove and serve immediately, with powdered sugar or jam or, if something more savory is desired, with sausages.

FUSSY NO MORE

When I was seventeen or eighteen, and cooking often, certain kinds of recipes seemed to stand for real cooking to me. I would make things such as *Salzburger Nockerl* and *baklava* with 50,000 layers. That fastidious precision seemed appropriate then. Sometimes my sister and I would make incredibly tiny pancakes, the size of a penny. You needed about 100 for a serving. My mother accused us of goofing off but, in that kind of fussy cooking, which I don't do very much any more, we were learning assiduously.

SANDWICHES

CREAMY MOZZARELLA SANDWICH

Serves 1

This started out as a lunch item, but since we eat bread in the morning and we eat cheese in the morning, it is entirely appropriate to combine them in this attractive sandwich. We can now buy mozzarella cheese that is not rubbery. As you only need two ounces per serving, splurge and get the very best you can find.

The sandwich is versatile. We serve it in the restaurant about three times a week, grilled and then baked. It can be open-faced or, what's the opposite, closed-faced? We serve it with black olives and sliced tomatoes drizzled with vinaigrette.

2 slices good-quality bread, preferably homemade (we use our Herb Bread, the recipe for which was in the first Cafe Beaujolais book)

About 1 Tbsp. olive oil

About 1 tsp. Pesto (see page 139)

About 1½ tsp. Dried Tomato Spread (see page 129)

About 2 oz. thinly sliced mozzarella cheese

Brush one side of each slice of bread with olive oil, then spread other side of each evenly with Pesto. (Use more if you want to.) Repeat with Tomato Spread. Be sure to go all the way to the edges of the bread slice so that every bite is delicious.

Pesto-side up, cover one slice of bread with cheese and top with other slice, Pesto-side down. Grill in a heated pan; flip when the underside is golden brown. If the cheese is not sufficiently melted when both sides are browned, place in a 400° oven for a minute or two.

WONDERING ABOUT WONDER BREAD

It seems obvious to me: if a person is given a choice of a freshly baked baguette or a slice of store-bought white bread, how could there really be a choice? And yet, in terms of dollar volume, white bread must outsell baguettes one hundred to one.

A few nights ago I went to a friend's restaurant—a wonderful little French restaurant in San Francisco. My friend was busy, so I sat in the back office reading cookbooks. A waitress arrived to start her shift and, while she was putting her stuff away, she discovered a loaf of supermarket white bread on top of the refrigerator. Now this restaurant makes what is easily one of the three most delicious breads I have ever eaten. They always have a ton of it around; there is never a shortage. The waitress determined that this white bread had been brought in by the person who washes the dishes. She got a real kick out of that. She asked him why he had brought it. He said, "Well, it's for sandwiches. I *have* to have this kind of bread." I sat there marveling. For me, it was as if someone had chosen to sleep on a bed of nails instead of a comfortable mattress. I concede that people must have their reasons, but I don't think I'll ever understand.

EGG SALAD SANDWICH

Serves 1

I'm just wild about eggs, despite their evil image of cholesterol and all that. I could eat them all day, every day. It took three tries of making this egg salad before I could get an outside opinion, because the first two times, I ate it all myself. Many people never think of it, but egg salad is a perfect way to eat eggs. If you don't feel like a conventional breakfast, you can have all the same ingredients, but in this very pleasant way, with an egg salad sandwich, on good bread, with lettuce and tomatoes and whatever else you choose to add.

The *Tofu* Dressing (see page 134) is an extremely healthy yet delicious addition to this dish.

If for any reason you don't want to use mustard, you can use something that I often put in egg salad: white vinegar. It gives it a little tang. And if you aren't going to serve it for a while, leave the walnuts out until it is time for assembly; otherwise they will become soggy.

2 eggs	¼ tsp. Dijon-style mustard or white vinegar
3 to 5 tsp. Tofu Dressing (see page 134)	⅛ tsp. salt
1 Tbsp. toasted walnuts, coarsely chopped	Freshly ground black pepper
	2 slices bread

Place the eggs in a small pan of cold water over high heat. Bring to a boil. Immediately remove from the heat and let the eggs sit in the water for 20 minutes. Remove the shells, mash the eggs with a fork, and add 2 to 3 tsp. *Tofu* Dressing, and the walnuts, mustard, salt, and pepper. Mix well and adjust for seasoning. Spread 1 to 2 tsp. dressing on slices of bread and proceed to make a sandwich.

OPEN-FACED SMOKED SALMON SANDWICH

Serves 1

In Mendocino, we have access to quantities of locally caught salmon. We feel compelled to come up with new ways to deal with said fish. We love responsibilities like this, especially when we get to experiment with smoked salmon. This is Chris's recipe, and it is a very simple one, but the addition of the lemon juice is what turns it from pretty good to great.

We smoke our own salmon by soaking it in brine, drying it under a fan, and then putting it in a hot smoker along with wood chips. We use a Little Chief smoker that we bought at the discount store for about sixty dollars. It's a dynamite little unit and easy to use, if you wish to try smoking your own.

2 slices good-quality bread, or one bagel cut in half	A few drops freshly squeezed lemon juice
4 Tbsp. (approximately) Herbed Cream Cheese (see page 132)	Freshly chopped dill
2 to 3 oz. smoked salmon	Freshly chopped parsley

Toast the bread or bagel. Spread Herbed Cream Cheese on both pieces. If the smoked salmon is dry, crumble it over the surfaces. If it is moist, slice strips and lay them over surface in a lattice design. Sprinkle with drops of lemon juice, then sprinkle with mixed herbs.

THE SNAKE MESSAGE

You think running a restaurant ever pales in interest? One morning, I found the message below, from our janitor, taped to my office door...

MARGARET —
I hope you aren't afraid of snakes, because there might be one in your office. It's a little one, I think it's injured. I was going to get it out but I waited and it moved and now I can't find it.

Makes 5 or 6 sandwiches

Chris and I enjoy thinking up new dishes, often during walks along the beautiful coastal headlands in Mendocino. One year, the lunch menu needed a new sandwich. We contributed suggestions for ingredients back and forth as we walked along, starting with smoked turkey, moving to creamy mayonnaise, adding nuts for texture, currants for sweetness, and our Rhubarb Glop for a tart relish. The resulting sandwich has been a hit at the restaurant, where it has been on the menu for more than two years.

The quality of the smoked turkey is of the utmost importance. Our meat contains no preservatives or weird fake smoke. The same recipe works well with other delicately smoked meats such as ham or pork. It's really easy to make, and people love it. We serve it on homemade whole wheat bread.

1⅓ cups Mayonnaise (recipe follows)
⅓ cup whole-grain mustard (we use Moutarde de Meaux)
½ cup currants, plumped in ½ cup tea for 15 minutes, then drained (we use black or Earl Grey)
2 lb. smoked turkey meat

Whole wheat bread
⅓ cup slivered, toasted almonds
1¼ cups young greens with a peppery flavor, such as arugula or watercress or even spinach
⅔ cup Rhubarb Glop (see page 30)

Mix together the mayonnaise, mustard, and currants and fold in the turkey. For each sandwich, place the turkey mixture on one slice of bread, sprinkle with toasted almonds and place greens over the meat so that they will peek out of the finished sandwich.

MAYONNAISE

Makes 2 ½ cups

2 cups corn oil
¼ cup vinegar (tarragon, rice, or sherry are good choices)

½ tsp. salt
2 tsp. Dijon-style mustard
1 whole egg + 3 egg yolks

In the bowl of a food processor fitted with a steel S-blade, or in a blender, place ¼ cup of the oil and all the other ingredients. Blend for just a few seconds. With the motor continuing to run, add the remaining oil slowly in a thin stream. The mixture will thicken by the time the last drop of oil is added, or a few seconds thereafter.

SOUPS

CHICKEN STOCK

Makes about 13 cups

In the first book, there was a chicken stock recipe that was very conventional: Put the parts in the water with vegetables and boil. This time I wanted something a little different, a little more ambitious, and a little more flavorful. I did that by baking the chicken parts for an hour, along with the vegetables. It gives the stock a deeper flavor.

The yield is a bit odd, but that's the way it turned out when I used what seemed a reasonable quantity of ingredients. I can't imagine going to all the trouble of making stock and making less than this. Stock has so many uses and can be frozen as well. Homemade stock is so much better than canned, I would never consider using the canned, which almost always is too salty and often contains MSG to boot.

By the term "jelly-roll pan," I mean a pan that has short sides: enough to keep the juices and fat from dripping all over the oven.

6½ lb. chicken necks and backs	4 stalks celery, cut into 1-inch pieces
3 yellow onions, peeled and coarsely chopped	2 bay leaves
4 carrots, peeled and cut into 1-inch pieces	2 tsp. salt
	5 cloves garlic, peeled
	2 cups loosely packed parsley

Preheat the oven to 425°. Wash the chicken parts with cold water and dry with paper towels. Place in two roasting or jelly-roll pans, about 1- by 15- by 1- or 2-inches. Distribute the vegetables around chicken parts and place the pans in the oven. Bake for 1 hour, stirring every 15 minutes to coat the vegetables with pan juices.

Transfer the contents of the pans to a large pot, add 6 quarts cold water and the remainder of the ingredients. Bring to a boil and skim the surface foam, which will continue to appear for about 15 minutes. Cover partially, so that steam can escape, and simmer for about 1½ hours. Pour through a strainer and remove fat with a large spoon. Refrigerate for several hours until the remaining fat has congealed and remove it.

THE ORIGIN OF GRANDMA KUMP

Chris Kump, my husband, specializes in the fancier cooking at the restaurant. His dishes usually appear at dinner. But he also has what I call his "Grandma Kump" persona. This has nothing to do with his real grandmother; it is *him* and his array of homier, more basic, simpler recipes. I can identify a Grandma Kump recipe from twenty paces. Now, whenever anyone else at the restaurant invents this kind of recipe, we bestow grandmahood on them, and call it Grandma Bob's, or Grandma Jeff's, or Grandma Morris's creation.

In my first book perhaps
the single most helpful
hint I offered was my
method for peeling garlic.
Now comes the prime can-
didate for most helpful
hint in this book: How do
you know where to cut
the lower end of a seven-
inch stalk of asparagus so
you don't have the part
that has the texture of a
whisk broom in your soup
or on your plate? The way
I was taught, which always
works, is to snap it. The
broomlike part won't
snap. Hold the two ends
and bend, and it will tell
you which part you want
by breaking in the proper
place.

GRANDMA KUMP'S LO-CAL ASPARAGUS, TARRAGON, AND GARLIC SOUP

Makes about 2 quarts

Whenever Chris cooks hearty, wholesome foods, we say that he is in his Grandma Kump mode, and the resulting recipe is entitled "Grandma Kump's" whatever. All he lacks at such times is the wig and dress. This is a great little Grandma Kump-style soup, because it is so low in calories, yet it tastes rich and delicious without the need for cream or butter.

During the months that asparagus is plentiful on the coast, it finds its way into many parts of the menu. The more attractive tips are used in salads, and the stems wind up in the soups. This actually could be turned into a "name your own vegetable" soup. Instead of asparagus, you could put in spinach, or broccoli, or cauliflower; two pounds of fresh *something*. Fresh tarragon is generally available about the same time of the year as fresh asparagus is.

¾ cup dry white vermouth
1½ cups Chicken Stock (see page 123)
3 cups water
1 lb. yellow onions, coarsely chopped
1 to 4 cloves garlic, coarsely chopped

¼ cup olive oil
2 lb. fresh asparagus (the middle stalks are fine, but snap off the fibrous white ends)
Salt and white pepper
2 Tbsp. fresh tarragon, minced

Place the vermouth, stock, and water into a large pot and bring to a boil. In a large skillet, sauté the onions and garlic in olive oil until soft (about 2 minutes). Add the asparagus and season well with salt and pepper.

Stirring constantly, continue to sauté over medium-high heat for 5 minutes, or until the asparagus is bright green and beginning to soften. Do not allow the onions and garlic to brown.

Empty the asparagus mixture into the pot containing the boiling stock, cover, and return to a boil over high heat, stirring occasionally. Continue boiling for 5 to 10 minutes, uncovered, just until the asparagus is softened. If you overcook it, the asparagus will lose its fresh, bright green color and become quite drab. Remove from the heat, purée, pour through a sieve, and add the tarragon and salt and pepper to taste. (If you don't care about calories, blend in up to ¾ cup of cream, or garnish with a dollop of lightly salted, whipped cream or sour cream.)

PUMPKIN AND TOMATO SOUP

Makes about 10 cups

I really like soup for breakfast, even when I don't have a cold (but I have been taking chicken soup with noodles in the morning for the cold I am battling as I deal with this section).

The nice thing about this recipe is that you use canned tomatoes and canned pumpkin, the same stuff you use to make pumpkin pie. It has a perfectly respectable flavor.

2 cups finely chopped onions	¼ cup finely chopped parsley
⅓ cup butter (or part corn oil)	1 Tbsp. honey
½ tsp. nutmeg	6 cups Chicken Stock (see page 123)
1 can (1 lb. 13 oz.) pumpkin	1 cup heavy whipping cream
1 can (14½ oz.) whole tomatoes, coarsely chopped	Salt and pepper to taste

Sauté the onions in butter for 10 minutes, until limp and translucent. Add the nutmeg, pumpkin, tomatoes, parsley, honey, and chicken stock and simmer for 5 minutes. Add the cream, purée, and season to taste. Serve with a dollop of lightly salted whipped cream or sour cream and a sprinkle of chopped parsley.

MMM, MMM GOOD

Soup for breakfast? Why not? Campbell did a whole promotion on this theme some years ago, and it made sense to me. Soup is comforting. People drink all manner of hot liquids for breakfast, and they eat tomatoes and vegetables in omelettes, so there again, the soup is just a reformulation of traditional breakfast ingredients into another incarnation.

SPINACH AND MINT SOUP *Serves 1*

ON FOOD MEMORY

A good food memory is useful in achieving consistency in the restaurant. If today's chicken broth isn't quite the same as last week's for whatever reason, I'll know. My food memory goes back at least twenty years, and that's more than enough.

When I've tried to recreate a recipe from something remembered from long ago, it often doesn't taste the way I remember it. Perhaps my memory *is* faulty—or perhaps it is the taste that changes, both literally and figuratively. Literally, because taste buds do age along with the rest of the body. And figuratively, because I'm no longer the person who loved that particular sauce on my tenth birthday dessert. Something that seemed utterly wonderful then might be an embarrassment now.

This topic can be a little disconcerting because I *do* have fabulous memories of things from my past, and sometimes I just can't recreate them in the kitchen.

One thing that's clear, though, is that food memories have little to do with influencing present-day tastes. I had a talk about this with Barbara Tropp. The question arose as to where seeds may have been planted that later flourished in *her* life. She came from a New Jersey Jewish background. Oriental eating consisted of canned *chow mein*. That could hardly have been the experience that turned her into a fabulous and innovative chef of Chinese cuisine.

My Mom makes a delicious spinach and mint salad, and it occurred to me one day that it could be turned into an excellent soup as well. This is not a soup that is going to change your life, but it is very fast and very simple, and the flavors have a nice zing, without demanding that your taste buds accept something dramatically off beat.

It is important to use only the leaves of the spinach, not the stem, so the rib down the center of each leaf must be removed. Of course the leaves must be well washed to remove the sand and grit.

1 cup Chicken Stock, preferably homemade (see page 123)
1 cup fresh spinach, ribbed and cleaned
1 to 2 tsp. chopped fresh mint
A few drops lemon juice

2 Tbsp. cubed tofu
2 to 3 Tbsp. cooked garbanzo beans
Salt and pepper
1 slice lemon

Bring the chicken stock to a boil. Reduce the heat slightly and add the spinach. Cook for about 30 seconds, then add the rest of the ingredients, except for the lemon slice, seasoning to taste. After 30 seconds, pour into bowl and garnish with the lemon slice.

SPREADS, SAUCES & DRESSINGS

DRIED TOMATO SPREAD

Makes about ½ cup

If you happen to love tomatoes, as I do, then you especially love the sweetness they have in season. For an all-too-brief period of time I am in heaven, tossing tomatoes into as many dishes as possible.

Dried tomatoes have lessened my seasonal withdrawal pains; they provide a delicious concentrated sweet flavor any time of the year. My favorites come from Karen Cox whose company, Just Tomatoes™, prides itself on using no sulfur or other odd additives (hence the name).

For this recipe, you can make your own dried tomatoes at home. The finished product is extremely versatile and will last for several months, covered, in the refrigerator. My dad happened to be heating some soup while I was testing the recipe, and some ended up in his soup where they were truly delicious. The next day, I used them in a salad. Subsequently, they have been mixed into scrambled eggs while they're cooking (looks good, too), used as an omelette filling, in biscuit dough, as a garnish, on a homemade pizza, as a sandwich spread, or on the end of a finger that has been dipped into the jar.

A word of caution: Use a small saucepan. Mine was too big the first time around, and I ended up with crackly blackened tomatoes on the bottom. The blackened vegetables trend has come and gone.

1 cup dried sliced tomatoes (about 1 oz.)	2 tsp. minced garlic
½ cup water	¼ cup olive oil

In a small pot, place tomatoes, water, garlic and 2 Tbsp. of the oil. Bring to a boil and cover, then turn the heat to low. Simmer gently for about 1 hour, until the tomatoes are extremely soft. Check frequently to make sure that the liquid has not evaporated. (If it has just evaporated, add up to 3 Tbsp. water; if the tomatoes are burnt, you can only throw them away.) Add the remaining 2 Tbsp. olive oil. Either purée in the bowl of a food processor fitted with metal S-blade to make a paste, or leave the tomato slices whole. Let cool completely, then cover and refrigerate.

CRANBERRY SAUCE

Makes about 2¼ cups

I don't like tart things when they are made too sweet, so I tend to keep them pretty tart. Cranberry sauce happens to be one of those things. If you prefer it sweeter, use the full cup of white sugar, or even a bit more. But it's very good the way it is here. The wine adds a depth of flavor that you rarely find in cranberry sauce. It makes it a more complex taste, yet it couldn't be any easier to make.

I wish fresh cranberries were available more of the year. When they are in the stores in the late fall, I buy quantities of them and freeze them for use all year.

Besides Thanksgiving, I serve this as a side dish for poultry or even pork all year round. I have mixed it with mayonnaise and used it as a sandwich spread; it is especially good in chicken and turkey sandwiches.

¾ to 1 cup white sugar	3 cups fresh or frozen cranberries
1 cup red wine	Grated zest of 1 orange
½ cinnamon stick	

In a saucepan, combine the sugar, wine, and cinnamon stick. Bring to a boil, stirring occasionally. Reduce the heat and boil gently for 3 minutes.

Discard any unsatisfactory looking cranberries and rinse the good ones. Add the cranberries and grated orange zest and simmer for 10 minutes. Remove from the heat and let cool. Remove the cinnamon stick.

CRÈME FRAÎCHE

Makes as much as you want

Sometimes I think that the two real staples of the restaurant kitchen are *crème fraîche* and Black Bean Chili. *Crème fraîche* is simply soured cream. One can buy it off the shelf in markets in France; here we have to make it ourselves.

It has a multitude of uses: straight on fruit; whipped, in soups; stirred into sauces. The thing that's so wonderful about it is that it doesn't break down when it's heated the way sour cream or yogurt does. It also has a mellower flavor—nutty, instead of tangy. You can whip it and make it thicker, the same way you do whipping cream, or you can use it in the more liquid stage.

Heavy whipping cream (as many cups as you wish)

Buttermilk (1 Tbsp. for each cup of cream)

Combine the cream and buttermilk in a saucepan over medium heat. Heat just until the chill is off—to about 90°. Pour into a glass jar, cover lightly with a piece of waxed paper, and let sit in a warm place (65° to 70°) for 12 to 20 hours, until the *crème fraîche* has thickened.

Replace the waxed paper with plastic wrap or a tight-fitting lid, and refrigerate for at least 6 hours before using. Keeps up to 2 weeks.

TESTING RECIPES

In testing recipes—my own or those from friends and from books—I have come to realize what a marvel it is that cookbooks ever get written, and that any of the recipes in them ever succeed. Getting it all down on paper, in proportions that really work, is extremely time consuming and exacting. I was pleased by the many letters from readers of my first book saying, with undisguised amazement, "But these recipes really *do* work." It bothers me that people are surprised. They must have had a lot of dreadful experiences.

Almost all of the testing for this book took place while my husband was on a long trip to Europe. So there was something funny about not having him to cook *for.* My Mom offered to hold a party to which lots of people would come and test things and fill out little questionnaires. But the problem is that there are so many things that just don't work well the first few times. I don't need anyone else to tell me that.

As I launched into a month of testing recipes at my parents' house, I declared that all sweet leftovers must be frozen instantaneously so that none of us would succumb to their lure. Well, that isn't quite the way it turned out, because frozen sweets can be quite wonderful straight from the freezer, without even waiting for anything to defrost.

HERBED CREAM CHEESE *Makes about 2½ pounds*

This is an all-purpose item that can be used equally well in omelettes, as a dip, on sandwiches, or to accompany raw vegetables. You can use good goat cheese in place of or in addition to the natural cream cheese.

We serve an herbed cream cheese omelette at the restaurant, and it's equally popular in the morning and for lunch.

1 Tbsp. chopped chives
3 Tbsp. chopped parsley
4 Tbsp. chopped green onions
  (white and green sections)
4 large cloves garlic, peeled
1½ Tbsp. vinegar (I prefer
  tarragon vinegar)

¼ tsp. freshly and finely ground
  black pepper
2½ lbs. natural cream cheese or
  fresh goat cheese, or a
  combination of the two

Place all the ingredients except the cheese into the bowl of a food processor fitted with a steel S-blade. Process for 15 seconds. Place the cheese in the bowl of an electric mixer. Add the herb mixture and beat thoroughly. The finished product lasts about a week in the refrigerator.

A tablespoon of the herb mixture alone (no cream cheese) can be added to ½ cup mayonnaise for use on sandwiches or hamburgers.

NUT OIL MAYONNAISE

Makes 2⅓ cups

I simply can't understand why anyone buys mayonnaise, when you can make something this good in about two minutes. Try this version for a variation on basic mayonnaise. The subtle flavor needs the addition of the nut of the oil you select. Otherwise, the flavor is a bit uncertain. It's great with a basic tuna salad and with cold artichokes. I'm aware that there are people who simply slather it on bread and eat it as is. Add the nuts just before serving or they will soften.

1½ cups corn oil	4 egg yolks
¼ cup white wine vinegar	½ cup walnut or hazelnut oil
½ tsp. salt	½ cup chopped, toasted
2 tsp. Dijon mustard	walnuts or hazelnuts

In the bowl of a food processor fitted with a steel S-blade, or in a blender, place ¼ cup of the corn oil and all the other ingredients except for the nut oil and nuts. Blend. With the motor running, add the remaining oils slowly in a thin stream. Mayonnaise will thicken by the time the last drop of oil is added. When you are ready to use mayonnaise, fold in nuts and proceed with your recipe.

THE SUPERSTAR VISIT

Many famous people come to Mendocino to get out of the limelight and most of them end up at Cafe Beaujolais. *They* may be relaxing, but it sometimes makes us a bit tense.

One morning, for instance, a very famous movie star came in. The people in the kitchen were nervous, hoping that no one would make a scene. No one did. The customers behaved with the greatest aplomb, although one lady did follow him outside to ask for an autograph.

He came back to ask me about a dinner reservation. (We were thankful that we had one table left.) While we were standing at the back of the restaurant chatting, a newly arrived customer grabbed his waiter, Howard Knight, and said, "Is that who I think it is?" Without missing a beat, Howard replied, "Yes, that *is* Margaret Fox."

CREAMY TOFU DRESSING, DIP, OR MAYONNAISE SUBSTITUTE

Makes about 2½ cups

I wanted to include this recipe because a lot of people wonder what to do with *tofu* (which is the polite name for soy bean curd, and which is increasingly available in mainstream supermarkets). This form of it is something that is eminently usable in a variety of different situations. In fact, we keep this around the house and are always finding new uses for it: as a salad dressing, a dip, or a sauce (it is really good on or with *jícama*). You can use it as a baked potato topping or as a pasta sauce. I've been using it as a mayonnaise substitute. In fact, it is used in the Egg Salad Sandwich on page 118.

For many people, the real selling point is that you can't tell that it is *tofu*, in part because the curry and the garlic and other ingredients give it a fine flavor. It is absolutely delicious and it couldn't be any simpler to make. The recipe calls for a pound of *tofu*, which is the amount that you usually find in a standard tub from the market. Get plain *tofu*, not any of the flavored kinds, and especially not apple-raisin *tofu*.

Ideally, this should be made the day before, in order to give the flavors a chance to blend. It tastes more *tofu*-ish (*to*-phooey?) right after it is made. It will keep in the refrigerator for at least five days.

The original inspiration came from a handout produced years ago by the late, lamented Consumers' Co-op in Berkeley, and my Mom just took off from there to create this.

¼ cup lemon juice
¼ cup vegetable oil
4 tsp. soy sauce
½ tsp. salt
¼ cup chopped yellow onion
4 green onions, about 8 inches long, finely chopped

1 or 2 cloves garlic; more if you like
⅓ cup packed chopped parsley
½ tsp. curry powder
16 oz. tofu, rinsed, drained, and dried with paper towels

Place all the ingredients except *tofu* into a blender or food processor and blend thoroughly. Add the *tofu* and blend until smooth.

SMOKED TURKEY SAUCE FOR WAFFLES

Serves 1

This recipe was inspired by a recipe from my 8th grade home ec. class for creamed chipped beef on toast (which I have chosen *not* to include in this book). But the idea of a savory sauce on baked dough must have been imprinted in my memory banks back then, to re-emerge later in life in this form.

I like the flavor of smoked turkey, but if one preferred, or couldn't find a smoked turkey, smoked pork or plain turkey will do. Sometimes I add mushrooms or other vegetables to this sauce as well. Be as flexible or creative as you wish.

½ cup white wine
1 tsp. finely chopped shallots
2 Tbsp. finely diced carrots
1 Tbsp. finely sliced celery
1 tsp. whole-grain mustard
½ cup heavy whipping cream
Pinch nutmeg
2½ oz. diced or slivered smoked turkey

½ cup thinly ribboned spinach (or green of your choice)
Salt and freshly ground black pepper or cayenne pepper if you want zip
1 waffle (such as the Whole Wheat and Wild Rice Waffles on page 85)

Place the wine, shallots, carrots and celery in a saucepan and cook until the wine is reduced by half. The vegetables should be tender. Add the mustard, cream, nutmeg, and turkey and cook over medium heat, stirring. The mixture will thicken after about 2 minutes. Then add the spinach. Stir until spinach is tender (about 1 minute). Taste for seasoning and pour over the hot waffle.

GOAT CHEESE PASTA SAUCE

Makes enough for pasta for 4

But then, of course, who knows what "pasta for 4" means? This subject precipitated a near brawl in the restaurant, all of the participants having firm and clear ideas, based on what they, or their families, or even acquaintances could or would eat. There is also the matter of time of day. Since many people are unaccustomed to pasta in the morning, they might eat less. Then again, they might eat more. I'd suggest starting with four ounces per person (dry or fresh) the first time, and see how it goes.

You can use any kind of goat cheese. I like Laura Chenel's California Chèvre because it is delicious and not too goaty. Be sure not to cook the sauce after mixing it with the pasta or else the ingredients will separate and the dish will look unappetizing.

4 Tbsp. pine nuts
8 oz. goat cheese
⅔ cup olive oil
1 Tbsp. minced garlic
¼ tsp. freshly ground black pepper
6 strips crisp bacon, crumbled

2 oz. grated dry cheese (Parmesan, Asiago, and/or dry Monterey jack)
12 cherry tomatoes (red and/or yellow), cut in half
1 Tbsp. minced fresh basil

Toast the pine nuts by putting them on a cookie sheet in a 325° oven for 10 to 15 minutes.

Mix together the goat cheese, oil, garlic, and pepper until smooth.

Cook pasta in boiling salted water, drain, and place in a large pan. Over medium heat, add the cheese mixture, the pine nuts, bacon, and grated cheese, and stir to combine and heat through. When ready to serve, mix in the tomatoes and divide among 4 heated bowls. Garnish with basil and serve.

SPICY SAUSAGE SAUCE

Serves 2

When a new business called Mendocino Pasta opened a few years ago, the owners asked for recipes from cooks in the area. This one ended up on the package of one of their varieties of pasta. One day, Chris, my husband, was making something with sausage in a cream sauce, and I thought it didn't look particularly appetizing. But then I tasted it. It was so delicious, and ever since, I've been hooked on the idea of combining sausages and cream, as I did in this recipe.

This is an extremely speedy recipe. You can actually make the sauce faster than you can make the pasta. The only responsibility you have is to find a sausage that's really good. Happily, superb sausages are finding their way into delicatessens and even supermarket deli cases. So please do not make this sauce with your basic baseball stadium specials.

2 Tbsp. olive oil	½ cup dry white wine
½ cup thinly sliced bell peppers	¾ cup heavy whipping cream
4 oz. sliced andouille or linguisa sausage	½ cup chopped green onions
¼ tsp. crushed dry red pepper	2 Tbsp. grated dry cheese
1 clove garlic, minced	Parsley

In a large skillet, heat the olive oil and add the bell peppers. Cook over medium heat for about 15 seconds and add the sausage, red pepper, and garlic. Cook 15 seconds more, add the white wine, and increase the heat to reduce the liquid by half. Then add the cream and cook for about 45 seconds, until slightly thickened. Add the onions and cheese.

Place cooked pasta in the pan and toss to coat with sauce. Divide into two warmed plates or bowls, sprinkle with finely chopped parsley, and serve at once.

TOMATO-EGGPLANT SAUCE

Makes about 1 quart

THE SANDY KOUFAX VISIT

Normally, we are very good about protecting and honoring the privacy of our famous visitors. But there was one exception. One of the waiters, Howard Knight, who has the tact of a butler, recognized the voice of the baseball star, Sandy Koufax, even though he could see only the back of Mr. Koufax's head.

Howard, normally a calm and composed fellow, controlled himself until he reached the kitchen, where he became quite excited. Manny, the chef on duty, shared his enthusiasm and begged Howard to go and ask for an autograph.

In a quiet, low-key manner, Howard approached Koufax, who graciously agreed. But while he was writing, Lynn, a waitress, who had been observing all of this with a jaundiced eye, pranced out from the kitchen and said, in not exactly a whisper, "Is this the line for autographs, then?"

Clearly she was not a Dodgers fan.

This wonderful sauce must be credited to Marcella Hazan; if it isn't exactly hers, it is very, very close. The main difference is that we bake the eggplant instead of cooking it on top of the stove. It requires a lot less attention that way and comes out just as good.

We use this recipe all the time *on* pasta, *in* pasta, in omelettes, as part of a filling, and as a filling and icing for the remarkable four-layered Catalan Omelette Cake (page 106). To give an idea of how much food even a small restaurant uses, our recipe in the restaurant is for sixteen times as much, and that's not a lot for us! Because it freezes really well, you might prefer to make a larger amount.

The only caution is to be really sure that the eggplant is well cooked. There is nothing even remotely worthwhile about crunchy eggplant.

1 lb. eggplant	½ tsp. red pepper flakes (the kind you shake on pizza)
¼ cup olive oil	
2 tsp. minced garlic	Salt and freshly ground black pepper
3 Tbsp. finely chopped parsley	
2 cups canned tomatoes	

Preheat the oven to 375°. Peel and dice the eggplant into ½-inch chunks, then sprinkle with 1 tsp. salt and allow it to drain in a colander for 30 minutes. Pat dry and place on a 10- by 15-inch rimmed baking sheet and mix with the olive oil. Spread evenly in the pan and bake until the eggplant is quite soft, about 1 hour. Stir frequently.

Pour off the oil into a heavy-bottomed pot and cook the garlic over low heat for about 3 minutes, stirring frequently. Add the parsley, tomatoes, and red pepper flakes and cook for 25 minutes. Stir in the eggplant and simmer for 5 more minutes. Taste for seasoning.

PESTO

Makes 1¼ cups

The heady fragrance of basil inspires me in the kitchen. To keep that inspiration all year round, make *pesto* ever present. I invent recipes just to find more excuses to use *pesto*. It is one of Italy's most magnificent contributions.

I like pesto in mayonnaise, salad dressings, on pasta, in butter, in soups, in salad dressings. I use it as an omelette filling with sour cream and cherry tomatoes. I spread it on bread slices before making grilled cheese and other sandwiches. I especially like it spread very thin on *croûtes* — little slices of baguette — that are then toasted and eaten directly or floated on soup. As I may have implied, I really like the stuff.

There is simply no point in wasting ingredients by making *pesto* with dried basil. *Pesto* freezes well, so I always make a great deal when fresh basil is plentiful. At the restaurant, we freeze it in 1-quart containers, but at home, ice-cube trays would be great; you can pop out just as much as you need.

There are many ways to make *pesto*. At the restaurant, we usually do it this way, but sometimes we leave out the cheese or the pine nuts.

2 cups firmly packed fresh basil leaves (stalks and stems are OK if you are using a food processor)

½ cup freshly grated dry cheese (Parmesan, dry Monterey jack or Asiago)

½ tsp. salt

2 large cloves garlic

½ cup olive oil

¼ cup pine nuts (optional)

Use a food processor fitted with a metal S-blade or a blender to combine all the ingredients until smooth. Store for up to 1 week in refrigerator or indefinitely in freezer.

THE JESSE JACKSON NON-VISIT

Jesse Jackson announced that he was bringing his presidential campaign to the Mendocino headlands to speak on Ocean Sanctuary. We may only have five hundred or so registered voters in Mendocino, but virtually every one of them is outspoken against offshore drilling on our coast.

Jackson's Secret Service people came to check us out. People at the restaurant were talking to people hovering in a helicopter somewhere up there. Then they scrutinized our lemon curd tarts and, using walkie-talkies to convey the particulars to others back at the headlands, ordered several. But the candidate didn't show up that day. He did come back to Mendocino a few weeks later, but we did not have the pleasure of his company.

SALSA

Makes about 2½ cups

Try as I may, I have yet to find any commercial *salsa* that I like as much as this one. Part of the reason is that fresh *salsa* really only lasts a couple of days, because the cilantro flavor dissipates, and it turns a funny color. Most importantly, though, it is impossible to duplicate the flavor of tasty fresh tomatoes. (Even a less than perfect tomato is better than a preserved one, and the use of a little tomato paste will overcome its imperfections.)

I have been seen in the kitchen eating this particular *salsa* by the spoonful; I won't deny it. But I'm not the only one. In the restaurant, the staff tends to put this *salsa* on everything from country fries to eggs to waffles to Creamy Polenta.

At Cafe Beaujolais, we're always a little tentative about making things too spicy, but that's difficult, because we all like spicy things so much. The hotness is, of course, adjustable by the quantities of *jalapeño chiles* that are added.

1 medium tomato, ripe and red	½ to 1 tsp. kosher salt
1 tsp. tomato paste (optional; use if the tomato is less than perfect)	⅓ cup chopped red onion
	¼ cup chopped green onion
2 Tbsp. white wine vinegar	¼ cup chopped cilantro
1 tsp. minced garlic	2 jalapeño chiles, seeded, stemmed, and minced
1 tsp. dried oregano (or 2 tsp. fresh if you have it)	

Chop the tomato. Combine the tomato paste, vinegar, garlic, oregano, and salt. Mix with all the remaining ingredients. Add up to 2 Tbsp. cold water if the *salsa* needs to be thinned. Use within 2 days.

PICO DE GALLO RELISH

Serves 4 to 5

We have used this relish at the restaurant to accompany our Black Bean Chili (see page 158). It's also good in anything in which beans are included, because it is quite a piquant garnish. It's very simple to make; just combine all the ingredients. You can improvise in adding other ingredients, such as celery or carrots or radishes, as you wish. The goal is to end up with something crunchy, set against the softness of the bean dish, and to be spicy and refreshing.

In the morning, you can also serve this relish with or on a wide range of egg dishes, from simple omelettes or scrambled eggs to more elaborate if unspicy creations.

Pico de gallo means "beak of the rooster" and of course you're pronouncing it "GUY-oh" and not like the name of the folks who sell wine.

¼ cup finely chopped red onion

2 oranges, peeled and thinly sliced crosswise (save the juice)

½ cucumber, cut in half lengthwise and thinly sliced (peel first if you wish)

½ jícama, peeled and cut into matchsticks

½ red bell pepper, cut into matchsticks

2 Tbsp. olive oil

1 Tbsp. white wine vinegar

Pinch salt, cayenne pepper, fresh oregano (or dried, if necessary)

½ tsp. crushed red pepper flakes

¼ cup orange juice (from above oranges and/or others)

Mix together the onion, oranges, cucumber, *jícama*, and bell pepper in a large bowl. In a small container, blend the remaining ingredients and pour them over the contents of the large bowl. Adjust the seasoning as needed.

THE CAFE BEAUJOLAIS DUDE RANCH

On long winter nights, we've actually talked seriously about doing this kind of thing. There are some famous do-it-yourself restaurants, at which you not only select and trim your steak, but cook it over a grill and bring it to your table—and pay for the privilege. At the Cafe Beaujolais Dude Ranch, people would come into the kitchen and cook their own meals, and we would stand around supervising them.

Actually, on a very small scale we have done this in conjunction with cooking schools around the country, with an "externship" program. People have come and worked for between one and four weeks in our kitchen, to gain experience. One man, who read my first book and was planning a comparable restaurant back East, sent his chef out to work for us for a couple of weeks and see how we run the place. But it isn't as if we throw the kitchen doors open to the hordes who would come streaming in. Not yet, anyway.

I've reflected seriously on the notion of the "one-hour extern." People would get a pep talk and some advice from me, then come into the kitchen and make real omelettes, in real time, for themselves and, who knows, maybe even for other customers. Oh, I can just see the staff rolling their collective eyes when they hear about this; another of Margaret's harebrained schemes!

A BUNCH OF SALAD DRESSINGS

Last August, we were so busy at times in the restaurant that we actually made ten gallons of salad dressing one morning, for use over the next few days. I wouldn't encourage you to do quite that much, although it does keep well. How about enough for a couple of weeks at a time? It saves time and even encourages more salad eating.

Salad dressings require the finest quality oils and vinegars. Spend a little more and buy a delicious olive oil; you will never be without it in the future. I generally stick with olive or corn oil in my dressings. My father-in-law, Peter, prefers safflower; he thinks it has a better taste than corn. You can buy herb-flavored vinegars, such as tarragon vinegar, but it is fun to experiment with making your own. They are extremely easy to do (and make lovely kitchen gifts as well, by the way).

It is challenging to match the salad ingredients to the dressing, but of course there is no right or wrong; do whatever seems appropriate to you. We have served a salad of Belgian endive and toasted walnuts, for which a dressing with walnut oil was really great. Chris makes a smoked pheasant salad with toasted hazelnuts and fresh poached pears. The dressing for that contains hazelnut oil that gives it an intensity that probably could not be accomplished in any other way.

VINAIGRETTE

Makes about 2⅔ cups

½ cup herb-flavored white wine vinegar (recipe follows) or sherry vinegar
2 Tbsp. Dijon-style prepared mustard

1 tsp. minced garlic or 1 clove peeled garlic on a toothpick (recipe follows)
1 tsp. salt
Freshly ground black pepper
2 cups oil (I use half olive, half corn)

Mix all the ingredients together. (I use a jar with a well-fitting top.) Adjust seasoning. Shake before using.

HERB-FLAVORED VINEGAR

Place the fresh herb of your choice in a clean jar. Tarragon and basil are my two favorites. Heat white wine vinegar and pour into the jar over the herb. Cover tightly and let it stand in a cool dark place without shaking for 3 weeks. Then strain the vinegar to remove the herb.

HAZELNUT OR WALNUT OIL DRESSING   *Makes 1 cup*

¼ cup freshly squeezed lemon
    juice
½ cup hazelnut or walnut oil

¼ cup corn oil
Salt and freshly ground black
    pepper

Whisk together until combined.

GOAT CHEESE DRESSING   *Makes 1¼ cups*

3 oz. goat cheese

1 cup vinaigrette (see page 142)

Purée until smooth.

YOGURT-CURRY DRESSING   *Makes 2½ cups*

2 cups plain yogurt
2 Tbsp. orange juice
⅓ cup olive oil
1 Tbsp. curry powder
Scant ½ tsp. cayenne pepper

1 Tbsp. honey
1 tsp. finely grated packed
    orange peel
Salt and freshly ground black
    pepper

Whisk together until combined. This one is good on fruit salad, too.

SALADS

CHRIS'S WALDORF SALAD and MARGARET'S WALKING SALAD

People with childhood memories of Waldorf salad will find this a more sophisticated rendition. But there are times when I hark back to the recipe from my Girl Scout days (Troop 2183, El Cerrito, California) for Walking Salad (although I've gussied it up a bit). Who says you can't go home again? You simply take a different route.

These salads should be made shortly before they are needed, or the apples turn brown.

CHRIS'S SALAD

Serves 3 to 4

4 apples
2 Tbsp. lime juice
1/3 cup currants
1/2 cup thinly sliced celery

2/3 cup Orange-Lime Mayonnaise (see below)
2/3 cup coarsely chopped toasted walnuts

Core the apples, cube (about 3/8 inch), and toss in a bowl with the lime juice. Add the currants, celery, and mayonnaise and mix to coat evenly. Add the walnuts just before serving.

Orange-Lime Mayonnaise

1 cup corn oil
Finely grated zest of 1 orange and 1 lime
1 Tbsp. orange juice, strained

1 Tbsp. lime juice, strained
1 tsp. Dijon-style mustard
1/4 tsp. salt
2 egg yolks

In the bowl of a food processor fitted with an S-blade, place 1/4 cup corn oil and the rest of the ingredients and blend. Then, with the motor running, add the remaining oil very slowly. Mayonnaise will thicken by the time all the oil is added.

MARGARET'S WALKING SALAD

Mix a little finely grated orange zest into cream cheese or ricotta, spread on an apple half and dot with raisins and a few toasted walnuts. Eat on the go.

Olive oils have pro-
liferated in recent years,
both in the number of
brands and the number of
varietal types. The most
important thing is the
taste. If it tastes good to
you, it's just fine. Some
people will end up prefer-
ring Extra Virgin and other
expensive kinds; others
will be pleased by the ordinary garden variety of
oil. I happen to like the
fruitier (and generally
more expensive) kinds.

RED AND GREEN COLESLAW WITH ORANGE DRESSING

Serves 6 to 8

Consider the notion of a morning picnic: quite appealing and out of the ordinary. So too is this coleslaw, dressed with vinaigrette instead of the more common mayonnaise. It is quite attractive, because it has both the colors of the cabbage, the white of the *jícama*, the black of the poppy seeds, and the orange of the orange juice. It is the sort of thing that would work well at a brunch too.

The ingredients should be readily available anywhere, although there may be a few parts of the world where *jícamas* (a crunchy Mexican tuber pronounced "HICK-a-ma") have not yet penetrated. They really are widely distributed; it's just that a lot of people don't recognize them in the supermarket, or know what to do with them. So ask, if you don't see them.

Finely grated zest of 1 orange
1/4 cup freshly squeezed orange
   juice
1 Tbsp. lemon juice
1/3 cup light olive oil
Salt and freshly ground black
   pepper

1/4 head each red and green
   cabbage, shredded
1/4 jícama, peeled and cut into
   matchsticks
2 Tbsp. poppy seeds
2 oranges, segmented

Mix together the orange zest, orange and lemon juices, olive oil, salt and pepper. In a separate bowl, combine the cabbage and *jícama*; add the dressing and poppy seeds. Toss. Taste for salt and pepper. Carefully add the orange segments and serve.

CITRUS SALAD

Serves 4 to 6

This is a salad that I grew up with. My mom made unusual and exciting salads frequently during my formative years, and I still find these flavors tangy, sweet, and refreshing. There are a lot of different flavors here—the citrus, the olive oil, the vinegar and the onion—and they all go together so nicely.

Neatness counts here. The orange and grapefruit segments must be pristine. I am annoyed when people say they don't have the time to remove the pith (the white stuff). When I was on the staff of the Great Chefs of France Cooking School, I was working with Michel Guérard, a three-star chef. He had me segment an entire case of grapefruit, and any imperfect ones were sent back for me to do again. The pith not only looks ugly, but is bitter as well. Household hint: The pith is much easier to remove if the unpeeled fruits are boiled for about a minute.

This salad could go very nicely with something sweet, such as the Black and White Soufflé (page 174).

1 head young Romaine lettuce	1 clove minced garlic
½ cup light olive oil	1 tsp. Dijon-style mustard
2 Tbsp. sherry vinegar or Japanese rice vinegar	1 small red onion, sliced thin
Salt and freshly ground black pepper	1 grapefruit
	1 navel orange

Wash and dry the lettuce leaves thoroughly and place them in the refrigerator. Prepare the vinaigrette by mixing together the olive oil, vinegar, salt and pepper, garlic, and mustard. Add the sliced onion and marinate for up to 4 hours.

With a very sharp knife, slice the entire peel and the white pith from the outside of the grapefruit. As you hold the peeled grapefruit in your hand, the sections should be apparent. Remove the individual wedges by cutting toward the center on both sides of each piece of membrane. The wedges should come out fairly easily and intact. Repeat the procedure with the orange.

When ready to serve the salad, toss the lettuce lightly with vinaigrette, add the citrus segments, and garnish with the marinated red onion rings.

The restaurant business,
for me at least, hasn't
been all that lucrative, although I'm doing better
than the 35 cents an hour
that I earned in the early
years. My first cookbook
not only afforded another
source of income, but it
brings people into the
restaurant and puts my
name before the public.
What's so nice is that you
don't have to write the
book every day, but you
do have to make the
omelettes every day.
    I like being a very
minor celebrity; people
tend to associate me, or
at least my name, with
something that is
pleasant. I don't have to
worry about adoring
throngs following me
down the sidewalk, or
about seeing my picture
on tabloids at the super-
market checkout stand,
but I do enjoy the meet-
ings and conversations
and events that occur be-
cause of the people who
do know the restaurant,
or me.
    It often seems nec-
essary to do things out-
side of the kitchen, or
the restaurant, or Men-
docino itself, to keep the
restaurant on people's
minds. That's why I teach
classes, and do pro-
motional events with
wineries, and cooking de-
monstrations at depart-
ment stores, and
contribute recipes to utility company newsletters.
Often it is enjoyable and,
undeniably, it helps keep

PAM MICHELS'S FAMOUS FRENCH POTATO SALAD

Serves 6

Potatoes should be one of the four basic food groups. Maybe it could occupy the fifth all by itself. One morning before noon, after a few days of potato-recipe testing, my mother's eyes glazed over, and she confessed, "You're reacting to what happened in your childhood, when I deprived you of potatoes." One lone tuber would have to suffice for the four of us. I played with Mr. Potato Head more than most kids did. Obviously, I am making up for lost time. Many years ago, my friend Pam Michels, a talented cook, developed a potato salad with vinaigrette dressing instead of mayonnaise; hence the Frenchness.

I've been eating this wonderful potato salad for the past four days. It *is* good and it's easy as pie to make. The important thing is to dress it while the potatoes are still warm.

If you are going to refrigerate the salad, plan to add quite a bit more salt and pepper, because the cold tends to stifle the flavor. I would normally serve this at room temperature, but I can tell you that it was awfully good for breakfast this morning right out of the refrigerator.

2½ lb. red potatoes (similar in size)	½ cup olive oil
1 tsp. salt	¾ cup minced green onions
Freshly ground pepper	¾ cup minced parsley, firmly packed
2 Tbsp. Dijon-style mustard	3 hard-boiled eggs, chopped (optional)
3 Tbsp. red wine vinegar	
1 clove garlic, minced	

Place the potatoes in a large pot, cover with cold water and bring to a boil. Continue cooking until the potatoes are easily pierced with a fork, 5 to 20 minutes depending on size. Remove from heat, drain, and let sit until warm (about 15 minutes).

Meanwhile, combine all the other ingredients except for the optional eggs.

Cut the warm potatoes into cubes, place in a large bowl, and add the dressing. Mix carefully; rough handling will result in mashed potato salad. Adjust for seasoning. Mix again every half hour. When ready to serve, taste again for seasoning. If refrigerated, it may require more salt and pepper. Add the eggs, if desired, just before serving.

PASTA SALAD

Serves 6 to 8

I nearly didn't include this because pasta salads have been done to death over the last few years. But just yesterday I ate it for breakfast after my early morning aerobics class and found it very satisfying. I wasn't hungry for hours. It does have a place after all.

The sky is the limit on additions, subtractions, and variations. Depending on how much of your meal you want this pasta salad to occupy, you can keep it fairly simple, or amplify it by adding crumbled *feta* cheese, tomatoes, and Greek olives (the really tasty ones; not the bland ones you stick on your fingers and wave around at birthday parties). Serve it on a bed of lettuce and you have an entrée.

The most important thing is to cook the pasta properly. What that entails is not dumping it in the boiling salted water and walking away. Test it often and drain it when it is neither too hard nor too soft.

The salad can be refrigerated, but I think it is even better at room temperature, never having been refrigerated. Alternatively, there is no reason why it can't be served warm. To do that, preheat all the ingredients except the cheese, then mix everything including the cheese together and serve in warm bowls.

Cafe Beaujolais in the public consciousness.

I used to worry about what I could possibly *say* to people. One often tends to forget, whatever one does in life, how much you really know, that other people *don't* know—or are at least interested in seeing how you work, even if it's only scrambling eggs.

1 lb. dried pasta in a shape other than long and flat (my favorite is the corkscrew-shaped fusilli)
⅔ cup olive oil
Salt and pepper
1 Tbsp. lemon juice
2 Tbsp. balsamic or sherry vinegar
1 tsp. minced garlic
2 Tbsp. finely chopped fresh basil

Finely grated zest from 1 lemon
½ cup finely chopped green onions
⅓ cup toasted pine nuts
½ cup grated dry cheeses (Asiago, dry Monterey jack, or Parmesan)
3 Tbsp. minced chives
½ cup finely diced red bell pepper

Cook the pasta in boiling salted water until tender, but not mushy (about 8 to 10 minutes). Drain and transfer to a large bowl. Mix together the oil, salt and pepper, lemon juice, vinegar, garlic, basil, and lemon zest in a separate container, then toss with the pasta. Let cool, then add the remaining ingredients, and adjust seasoning.

PIZZA & SALAD ↑

FULL SERVICE DINING →

ENTRÉES

BASIL CHEESE STRATA

Serves 6

Strata means "layers" and a *strata* can be made of layers of anything at all. This particular *strata* might be thought of as a glorified cheese sandwich or perhaps a glorified bread pudding. It got the rest of its name because of the basil in the *pesto*.

It is warm and comforting, and you can add almost anything to it. The point of a *strata* is that the whole is more than the sum of its parts; that is, the finished dish seems more interesting than the main ingredients. You can achieve this by adding, for instance, lightly sautéed green onions, sun-dried tomatoes, sliced cooked spicy sausage, or garlic.

I've made this with all kinds of bread. A homemade baguette was not as satisfactory as were some of the commercial breads; the slices were too small. I use the bread, crust and all, partly because I really like crusts, and partly because I like to use up all my leftovers.

3½ Tbsp. softened butter
8 slices dry bread, with crust
    (enough to cover 2 layers of
    an 8-inch-square pan)
6 oz. grated sharp Cheddar
    cheese
5 eggs, beaten

¼ tsp. Tabasco sauce
2¼ cups milk
⅛ tsp. white pepper
½ tsp. salt
1½ Tbsp. Pesto (see page 139)

Butter the pan lightly. Spread the remaining butter on one side of each slice of bread and place one layer of bread in the pan, buttered-side up. Sprinkle with the grated cheese. Cover with the remaining bread.

Whisk together all the remaining ingredients and pour over bread and cheese. If additional ingredients are going in, they should be included in one of the layers. Push the top layer of bread down into the egg mixture to make sure that all the slices are coated. Cover with plastic wrap and refrigerate for at least 6 hours or overnight.

Preheat the oven to 350°. Remove covering and place in the upper third of the oven. Bake for 30 to 35 minutes, until puffy and brown. Let stand 5 minutes before serving.

The *strata* can be reheated by wrapping it in foil and placing it in a preheated 350° oven for 15 minutes.

The carryout window is going well, and not just for coffees and cakes. People will come up and order a stack of paper plates full of omelettes and everything else on our menu. Much in the presentation and ambiance is lost that way, but the food travels fairly well, if it is only a short trip back to the hotel or motel. (No mail-order omelette requests, please.)

I have added a statement at the bottom of the menu that all food is available to go, at no extra cost, whether at breakfast, lunch or dinner. I have hopes that this will expand our take-out business from the two or three percent of the total it now represents. I've never understood why some restaurants charge more for take-out. Without overhead, waitress time, or dishes to wash, if anything it should be less.

TEX-MEX CORNBREAD PUDDING

Serves 4 to 6

A cornbread surplus haunts Cafe Beaujolais. Leftover muffins accumulate in the freezer. Once, when things reached a danger point (90% of the freezer was filled with muffins), Chris developed this recipe to deal with the problem.

It resembles a *strata*, a layered affair of cheese, custard, bread, and seasonings. It can be the main food element in a morning food assemblage, either by itself, or with something like Black Bean Chili.

You start with the Corn Bread recipe on page 62 and turn it into croutons. With a good knife, you can do this when the bread is really fresh, if you wish. (The croutons may also be used in other dishes, such as duck salad or a black bean soup. Both the color and the texture are wonderful.) Don't despair about the apparent quantity of croutons; they will shrink in the browning process as the moisture leaves them.

You can toast the oregano at the same time as you're toasting the croutons, but only leave it in for 5 to 8 minutes. It will tell you when it is done by its strong oregano odor.

Roasted red peppers are available as a commercial product, in jars or cans. If you can't find these, you can use ordinary red bell peppers, thrown in uncooked. Or you can use chopped pimientos. They're there as much for the color as the taste.

This dish takes to reheating really well, so you can make it the day before and refrigerate it.

Half of the Corn Bread recipe (page 62) (Make the entire recipe, then use half the bread for this)
4 eggs
2 egg yolks
1 tsp. turmeric
3 cups warm milk (regular or low-fat)
¼ cup finely chopped fresh jalapeño peppers

½ cup chopped roasted or fresh red bell peppers
½ cup finely chopped green onions
1½ tsp. salt
2 tsp. oregano (toasted at 300° for 5 to 8 minutes)
¼ tsp. Tabasco sauce
1½ cups (6 oz.) grated Monterey jack cheese

Preheat the oven to 300°. Make corn bread croutons by cutting the corn bread into ¾-inch cubes. Spread out in a single layer on a 10- by 15-inch pan and toast for about 45 minutes until dry and lightly browned. Stir occasionally to avoid burning. When brown, place in a single layer in a lightly buttered 8-inch-square pan. They should cover the entire bottom. Turn oven up to 375°.

In a large bowl, place the eggs, egg yolks, and turmeric and beat until well blended. Add the milk, whisk and add the remaining ingredients except the cheese. Sprinkle the cheese evenly onto the layer of croutons, then pour the liquid over the cheese. If any croutons pop to the surface, poke them down to be sure they soak up the custard.

Carefully place the 8-inch pan into a larger one. Pour boiling water into the larger pan about halfway up the sides. Bake for 45 minutes or until set in center. When a knife inserted in the center comes out clean, pudding is ready.

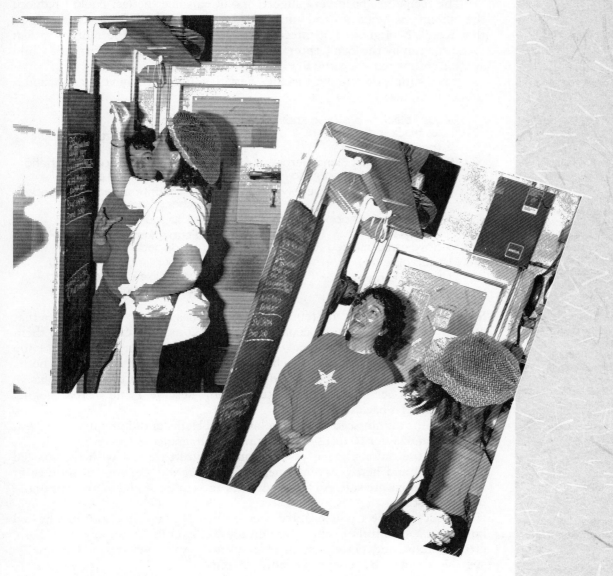

BLACK BEAN CHILI
Serves 8 generously

I simply couldn't omit this favorite recipe even though it appears in my first book, *Cafe Beaujolais*, as well. It has long been a mainstay of our existence and, except for the waffles, it remains our most popular dish, appearing in omelettes, as an essential part of other concoctions, or by itself in a bowl with cheese, sour cream, and cilantro.

The recipe has been very slightly modified since the last book: I reduced the amount of *jalapeño* (and corrected the placement of the accent mark in that word). It originated at Greens, the famous vegetarian restaurant in San Francisco run by the Zen Center, and we are forever indebted. Even Julia Child ate this chili when she came to visit a few years ago.

It is a simple dish to put together, very flavorful, entirely vegetarian, and it freezes well, too.

4 cups black beans (also known as black turtle beans)	1 tsp. salt
2 Tbsp. cumin seed	3 cups canned, crushed whole tomatoes
2 Tbsp. Beaujolais Blend Herbs (see page xv) or oregano	1/3 cup finely chopped jalapeño chiles (canned are fine)
2 large finely chopped yellow onions	1/2 lb. Monterey jack or Cheddar cheese, grated
1½ cups finely chopped green bell peppers	2/3 cup sour cream
1 clove garlic, minced (optional)	1/2 cup green onions, finely chopped
1/2 cup olive oil	8 sprigs cilantro (and, if you really like cilantro, 2 Tbsp. more to sprinkle on top)
1 tsp. cayenne pepper	
1½ Tbsp. paprika	

Sort through the beans and remove the funky ones and the small pebbles that are always there. (Our prep cook doesn't like doing this either.) Rinse them well. Place in a large pot and cover with water to several inches above the top of the beans. Cover and bring to a boil. Reduce the heat and cook for 1¾ hours or until tender. You will need to add more water if you start to see the beans.

When the beans are cooked, strain them. Reserve 1 cup of the cooking water and add it back to the beans.

Place the cumin seed and Beaujolais Blend Herbs or oregano in a small pan and bake at 325° for 10 to 12 minutes until the fragrance is toasty.

Sauté the onions, green peppers, and garlic in the oil with the toasted cumin seed and herbs, cayenne pepper, paprika, and salt for 10 minutes or until the onions are soft. Add the tomatoes and chiles. Add this mixture to the beans and stir.

To serve, place 1 ounce grated cheese, then 1¼ cups hot chili in a heated bowl. Put a spoonful of sour cream on top of the chili. Sprinkle with 1 Tbsp. green onions, and place a sprig of cilantro in the sour cream. Optionally, sprinkle about 1/2 tsp. chopped cilantro on top.

CHINA MOON SHANGHAI RICE[1]

Serves 3 to 4

LEAF, LOAF, AND LADLE

In my first book, I mentioned that my childhood fantasy was to open a salad, bread, and soup restaurant called *Leaf, Loaf, and Ladle.* I offered that name to the world, no royalties. A friend took me up on the offer, as it were, and sent me a published article of his called "Leaf, Loaf and Ladle." There was only one small problem. His recipe for Bacon Salad lacked the bacon. On the copy he sent me he had pencilled it in.

Barbara Tropp is the chef and owner of China Moon Cafe in San Francisco and the author of definitive books on Chinese cooking. She comes to Mendocino and stays with us for a respite from her hectic life in the city. Her dishes all have excellent flavors and are extremely satisfying. She writes, "Here is a wonderfully warm and soothing rice dish, very colorful and redolent of smoked bacon. A simple Cafe Beaujolais omelette or scrambled eggs would be the perfect accompaniment."

1 cup short- or medium-grain rice
3 Tbsp. tiny cubes smoked bacon, fatty bits included[2]
1½ tsp. kosher salt[3]
1 Tbsp. (approximately) corn or peanut oil
⅓ cup thinly sliced shallots
1 Tbsp. Chinese rice wine or dry sherry

One or more of these garnishes:
thinly cut green and white scallion rings
finely diced red bell peppers or red Fresno chiles
finely julienned carrot
finely julienned snow peas
blanched hearts of baby Chinese cabbage

Wash rice repeatedly in several rinsings of cold water until the water runs clear. Drain well.

Put the bacon in a small skillet, add ⅛ inch water, then bring to a simmer and cook until the cubes seize up and render some fat, about 2 minutes. Drain the juices into a cup measure and add enough hot water to equal 1½ cups. Add the salt and stir to dissolve.

Heat a heavy 2- to 2½-quart saucepan over moderate heat until hot. Glaze the bottom with oil, add the shallots and bacon, then stir gently until shallots are golden and very fragrant, adjusting the heat so that they sizzle without scorching. Add the wine, stir about 10 seconds to burn off the alcohol, then add the rice and stir to mix.

Add the salted bacon water to the pan, stir well to combine, and bring to a simmer. Cover, reduce heat to the lowest possible setting (if using an electric stove, transfer the pot to a preheated low burner) and cook for 20 minutes without lifting the lid. Remove the pot from the stove and let it sit undisturbed for another 20 minutes.

Remove the lid, fluff the rice gently with spatula to loosen it, then stir in the scallion and peppers or other garnishes, reserving some to sit prettily on top.

---

1. ©Barbara Tropp, all rights reserved. Adapted from the *China Moon Cookbook* (Workman, in press).

2. Any good quality bacon, *pancetta*, or crumbled pork sausage may be used.

3. If you have sea salt or table salt, use only half as much. Kosher salt is exceedingly mild and its flavor is best here.

TOASTED SESAME OIL

I've found toasted sesame oil in many supermarkets, often in an oriental foods section. Of course I realize I live in a somewhat rarefied world here in northern California, as far as gourmet or ethnic foods are concerned. But this isn't like needing seventeen kinds of radicchio or some rare Peruvian mushroom. It's a basic ingredient of oriental cooking. Can you find it in your standard supermarket in Boise or Wichita? Goodness, I hope so. The oil is heavy and rich, with a deliciously deep toasty flavor. It can be used happily in scrambled eggs, or to drizzle on a Chinese chicken salad.

This recipe was inspired by fond memories of the best Chinese noodle dishes I have ever tasted, those offered by my friend, Barbara Tropp, at her China Moon Cafe in San Francisco. It offers the opportunity to combine five of my favorite ingredients in one dish: peanut butter, *chile* peppers, noodles, sesame oil, and soy sauce.

People really go wild for this dish. At the restaurant, we serve it cold, both the noodles and the sauce. As for the origin of the unusual name, the story goes like this: Someone said, "What should we call this?" I said, flippantly, "Oh, I don't know . . . how about Bun Bun Noodles?" That day, I actually had a bit of spare time and made one of my rare strolls through the dining room. People kept asking me for the recipe. Later, I ran into one couple on my way to the post office. They reported that they hadn't stopped thinking about those Bun Bun Noodles.

It was offered as a lunch item at the restaurant, but it is clearly a morning food. I mean, people do eat peanuts on their sticky buns or in their granola, and flour in any number of ways, and all we're doing here is recombining the ingredients into this marvelous dish.

10 oz. dry pasta—spaghetti or angel hair

¼ cup smooth peanut butter (the least adulterated kind available)

3 Tbsp. sugar

¼ cup low-salt soy sauce

1 tsp. chile pepper flakes

3 Tbsp. toasted sesame oil

1 Tbsp. minced garlic

3 Tbsp. corn oil

Garnishes: slivered carrots, green onions, red peppers, toasted sesame seeds, roasted peanuts, fresh cilantro

Cook pasta in a large pot of boiling salted water until done, then drain and rinse with cold water until the noodles are cold. Let noodles drain for about 10 minutes.

Whisk together the rest of ingredients until thoroughly blended. (You could heat the mixture very slightly to facilitate whisking, or set the bowl over the steam rising from the cooking pasta for a few minutes.) Toss the noodles with sauce.

Let stand at room temperature for at least 4 hours before serving, or refrigerate and serve within 2 days. Always toss noodles before serving to distribute sauce evenly.

To serve, place a mound of noodles on plate and garnish with your choice of any or all of the pretty, crunchy additions listed above.

JUDY'S "INSTANT PIZZA" *Makes 1 or 2 servings*

Judy Carrell was an engaging waitress and charming person at the restaurant for many years. A couple of years ago she and her talented husband, Paul, just upped and moved to Tortola in the Virgin Islands, and we miss them desperately. For a while they ran a charter boat operation: he was the captain and she the cook. People expect great food on these charters, so Judy had to come up with a lot of wonderful recipes that can be made quickly and easily in a tiny ship's galley. This is one of them.

I know there are many people who enjoy cold pizza for breakfast, but I am not one of them. However, this recipe has persuaded me that hot pizza for breakfast is quite an all right thing to do. As with so many dishes, it can be as laden as you wish, with mushrooms or other vegetables, and even with a fried or poached egg on it.

1 whole wheat pita bread	A few rings of red onions
1 Tbsp. Pesto (see page 139)	1 cup grated cheese (tangy Cheddar is Judy's favorite and mine)
1 tsp. Dried Tomato Spread (see page 129)	
1 Tbsp. finely chopped olives, the more flavorful the better	3 thin slices fresh tomato
	1 tsp. minced fresh parsley

Preheat the oven to 350°. Spread pita bread with Pesto and Tomato Spread. Sprinkle with olives. Place onion rings all over surface. Distribute the cheese evenly, then overlap the tomatoes to cover as much of the cheese as possible. Bake, uncovered, for 20 minutes. Remove from the oven and sprinkle with parsley. Cut into four pieces and serve.

ALPBACHER GRÖSTL

Serves 6 to 8

THE U.S. VERSUS EUROPE

It was an interesting jux-taposition: my husband spent six weeks eating his way through Europe while I was home testing the recipes for this book. When we finally got together, we each talked endlessly about our food experiences.

Even though he ate great food every single day, the Europeans don't make a big deal of it. It has to do with the quality of their life. Good food is a part of life. When French people I know are served something really crummy, they can't believe it has happened. It's like a flat tire. One acknowledges it *may* happen, but it is certainly nothing one expects more than once every year or two. Europeans take it for granted that the most common thing is going to be perfect: the baguette with the fresh unsalted butter and the superb coffee.

In America, all people seem to think about is food. People make such a deal of it. I've seen lines of twenty or thirty people waiting outside a fashionable cheese shop. They'll end up with very good cheese, to be sure, but it is not a routine purchase. It is more like worshipping at the altar of the great food gods.

There is an excessive cuteness and presumptiveness in the United States. In Europe, it is taken for granted that the vegetables will be fresh and the bread will be great, and you

Once, when my husband and his father were in Austria, James Beard, then dean of American gastronomy, visited them, and they prepared this version of an Austrian farmer's hash.

Normally I do not care for the flavor of caraway seeds, but they are absolutely essential here, giving the dish a smoky flavor. You can use other kinds of leftover meats, such as chicken or veal and, if you want to treat it as a traditional breakfast hash, you might wish to serve one or two fried or poached eggs on top or alongside.

2 lb. potatoes	1 medium onion, chopped
1 lb. leftover roast beef	2 tsp. caraway seeds
1 lb. smoked ham	Salt and freshly ground black
4 Tbsp. butter, vegetable oil, or	pepper
a mixture of the two	2 Tbsp. minced parsley

Boil the potatoes briefly until still firm but no longer raw and refrigerate until cold. Then cut into 1-inch cubes. Dice the roast beef and ham into ¾-inch cubes.

Fry the potatoes in a heavy-bottomed frying pan, using 3 Tbsp. of the butter, until golden brown, about 30 minutes. In a separate pan, sauté the onion in the remaining butter for 8 to 10 minutes, then add the caraway seeds, roast beef, and ham and cook for another 2 or 3 minutes. Season with salt and pepper. Combine all the ingredients but the parsley, adjust for seasoning, sprinkle with parsley, and serve.

TURKEY-FRIED HASH

It is a rare occasion when I offer to cook "for fun" outside the restaurant, but Thanksgiving is such an occasion, because it is my favorite holiday other than my birthday.

In recent years, Chris and I have gone to the home of Tricia Priano, the restaurant's extraordinarily talented manager and wine buyer, and her husband, Bob Lorentzen, author of *The Hiker's Hip Pocket Guides* to the northern California coast. When they told me that twenty-five people were coming to last year's festivities, I was relieved. This was a group I could cook for. So I baked a huge turkey and made the delicious stuffing from the first Cafe Beaujolais cookbook. Chris contributed some luxurious ingredients left over from his recent dinner preparations: Armagnac-soaked prunes and maple-glazed fresh chestnuts.

Even after stuffing this mammoth turkey and baking some of the stuffing in a pan, I still had more than a gallon and a half left over. So much for my measuring ability. In an attempt to use these leftovers in an imaginative way, I thought up a hash, and offered it the next day in the restaurant.

I had no idea whether my customers would have any interest in anything to do with turkey so soon after Thanksgiving, especially with the rather odd name I gave it, but they ordered all that we had in the first three hours. I give no quantities, because everything here is entirely flexible, depending on the quantity of *your* leftovers. As in so many recipes, there is ample opportunity to be creative, by adding or subtracting ingredients, as you wish.

Chunks of fresh pear	Cooked spicy pork sausage
Butter and vegetable oil	Fried eggs
Chopped roast turkey	Parsley as garnish
Leftover stuffing	

Sauté chunks of pear in butter. Mix together the turkey, stuffing, sausage, and pear. Make patties about ¾-inch thick, each from about one cup of the mixture. Melt some butter and oil, and when the fat sizzles, fry the patties until they are brown and crispy on both sides. Serve with or under fried eggs, and garnish with parsley.

don't have to use a thousand adjectives on the menu to tell people that.

Sometimes I wonder if we might be in transition as an eating society, from the simpler and blander foods of our parents and grandparents. Perhaps one day, while I'm still around to enjoy it, people will simply *expect* food to be excellent, and not feel the need to drive a great distance to get a certain kind of mushroom . . . and then be sure to let people know they paid $17.95 a pound for it. Of course as such a time approaches, it will be more and more of a challenge to keep Cafe Beaujolais ahead of the pack, as it were, so people will continue to regard it as a very special place.

SIDE DISHES

CREAMY POLENTA

Serves 4 or 5

Roberta Wright, a cook at Cafe Beaujolais, regularly amazes me with her ability to create things both simple and intricate. At one end of the scale, she is a fantastic baker, whose creations make our customers gasp. And at the other end, she comes up with simple homey preparations that also taste good. This creamy *polenta* is one of the latter. I'm a great cornmeal fan and I like all *polentas*, but the unexpected appearance of milk makes this one not only creamier, but also gives it an entirely different and very pleasing flavor.

In addition to being served as morning food, it could be used as the side starch with chicken stew, or whenever you would use potatoes.

5 cups liquid (at least 3 but up to 5 of milk; 2 or fewer of water or chicken stock)	¼ tsp. Tabasco sauce
	1 cup polenta
¾ tsp. salt	Topping of your choice (suggestions follow)

Bring the liquid to a simmer in a heavy-bottomed saucepan. Add the salt and Tabasco sauce, then pour the polenta into the liquid in a heavy stream, whisking constantly over medium heat for 5 minutes. Pour into warm bowls and add topping of your choice.

TOPPINGS

Maple syrup or brown sugar and milk: For a traditional breakfast, it is hard to imagine anything more comforting than creamy *polenta* with this topping. It is immensely satisfying. Think of it as the morning food equivalent of chicken soup. Come to think of it, I have eaten this in the evening when I've been ill, just as I've eaten chicken soup for breakfast. It all goes to show . . .

Mexican topping: Sprinkle *polenta* with 2 Tbsp. cheese, then drizzle 2 Tbsp. warmed *salsa* over the top. Garnish with chopped cilantro. You may wish to add a few tablespoons of Black Bean Chili (see page 158) to a bed of *polenta*, then these toppings.

Italian topping: Swirl 1 or 2 tsp. Pesto (see page 139) into the *polenta*, and sprinkle grated Parmesan cheese on top. Place in a hot oven for one minute to melt. If you want the morning food to be more substantial, consider adding some spicy Italian sausage links, cut into chunks, and/or some Tomato-Eggplant Sauce (see page 138).

Almost anything else under the sun: The taste of *polenta* is sufficiently mild that virtually any topping you can think of, from beef gravy to Rhubarb Glop, will probably work just fine.

Just kidding about the Rhubarb Glop.

MUSH

When I was little, my dad used to take my sister and me swimming at night at the Richmond Plunge. We would come back really late, about eight o'clock, completely famished. My dad would make cornmeal mush and we'd have it with milk and brown sugar on it. I still remember how delicious it was, in that time and place.

Cornmeal mush is also known as polenta. When I called it Mush on the menu, no one ordered it, so now it's Polenta. There are so many possible interpretations of this dish, ranging from something sweet and cereal-like to something more grainlike. You can turn it Mexican with salsa, or Italian with tomato sauce. I don't know why people eat polenta plain when it's such a wonderful carrier for other flavors.

CRUNCHY COUNTRY FRIES

Serves 1 to 2

People who come to the restaurant love our fried potatoes and they always ask, "What do you do to them?" The fact of the matter is that we really don't *do* much of anything. It is nothing I could easily make a recipe of, since all we do is boil red potatoes, cool them, slice them, and fry them in butter and oil on the grill. No seasonings, no nothing. The only thing you have to remember to do is cook them enough so that they are crispy.

Some people can't accept that; they assume there has to be something more special than just frying potatoes, just the way they do, or could, at home. Can it be the ambiance and mystique of the place that magically permeates the food? They say, "Oh, these potatoes are fabulous," when I think what they really mean is, "Oh, Mendocino, I love it here."

But we do have more potatoes up our sleeve, so to speak, than just the simple unadorned crispy fries. This recipe has a bit of pizazz. I call it *chez vous* (your place), because there are enough variations that you can end up doing it any way you want.

This recipe really works better in a, what's the opposite of a nonstick skillet . . . a stick skillet? Cast iron works well. They don't get crunchy enough in a nonstick pan. And take your time when you're making this. Things don't crisp up on demand, but with enough time they will.

When I was testing this recipe I wondered how many people it would serve. My mother (elsewhere in this book I reveal her strange relationship with the potato) said at least two. Then I reflected on the amount my husband eats, and the really scary amounts that some people in the restaurant eat, and I thought I'd better say *one* to two.

CRUNCHY COUNTRY FRIES CHEZ VOUS

3/4 lb. small red potatoes, unpeeled
1/4 cup butter, olive oil, or vegetable oil (or a mixture)
1 cup red onions, finely chopped
1/2 tsp. salt

Freshly ground black pepper
1 tsp. minced garlic
1 Tbsp. finely chopped parsley
1 Tbsp. sour cream

Parboil the potatoes until just tender, then drain them and refrigerate until thoroughly cold: several hours or overnight. Cut into cubes, about 3/4- to 1-inch square. Heat the butter and/or oil in a large skillet (*not* nonstick). Add the onions and sauté until soft, but not browned, about 10 minutes. Turn up the heat and add the potatoes, salt, pepper, and garlic. Use a spatula to combine the ingredients without mashing them. Cover the pan with a tight-fitting lid, turn the heat down and cook for about 10 minutes, turning the potatoes occasionally. Remove the lid and cook for another 5 minutes, or until potatoes are crispy on the outside.

To serve, transfer to plate and garnish with parsley and a blob of sour cream.

VARIATIONS

1. Add any or all of the following:

grated cheese (about 1 minute
    before serving)

sautéed mushrooms

cooked vegetable of your
    choice (my favorite is broccoli)

caraway seeds (at the same time
    that the potatoes are added)

salsa and sour cream (just before
    serving)

2. Make the Extravaganza version.

CRUNCHY COUNTRY FRIES EXTRAVAGANZA

This is one of the most delicious things we serve in the restaurant. Some people behave almost as if this dish were a minor light and airy accompaniment. They will eat the Extravaganza with chicken-apple sausage and eggs and a big helping of coffee cake. At such times, I want the waitress to ask these people if they have notes from their mothers.

Crunchy Country Fries, as above

⅔ cup sliced mushrooms

1 Tbsp. butter or olive oil

½ to 1 tsp. minced garlic

1 tsp. Beaujolais Blend Herbs
    (see page xv)

¼ cup finely chopped green
    onions

⅓ cup grated cheese

Sour cream garnish

Prepare the Crunchy Country Fries recipe. Sauté the mushrooms in butter, garlic, and Beaujolais Blend Herbs for about 3 minutes. Drain (save liquid for soups and such). About 2 minutes before the potatoes are ready, add the green onions to the potatoes and cook until the onions are limp. Add the mushrooms and grated cheese. Cover the pan to melt the cheese. When the cheese is melted, transfer to a plate and garnish with sour cream.

DESSERTS

EASY HOMEMADE YOGURT: REGULAR, CHOCOLATE, OR CARAMEL

Makes as much as you wish

Of course you can buy yogurt in any market, but you can also make it at home very, very easily, and exercise creativity in the use of exotic flavorings. You don't need a fancy yogurt appliance (although it helps to maintain the constant temperature that you need). My mom makes this all the time and it always turns out right. What I find so fascinating is that you need such an incredibly tiny bit of yogurt starter to create a new batch.

As much milk as you want,
    whole, low-fat, or nonfat
A little yogurt for starter
For chocolate yogurt: 1 generous
    Tbsp. Mom's Cocoa Syrup
    (page 202) or 1 oz.
    semisweet chocolate

For caramel yogurt: 6 caramels
    (Grand Finale buttercreams if
    possible)

Scald the milk to a temperature of 185°. Cool to 115° and strain into clean jars. For each cup of milk, add ¼ tsp. yogurt and stir well. Place tops on the jars and set into a water bath at about 115°. Cover the water bath container in order to hold in the heat as much as possible. You can drape a towel or put a lid over it.

Set the entire water bath in the oven (or any other place in which you can maintain a temperature of between 110° and 115°). If you have an electric oven, turn it on for between 30 and 60 seconds, then turn it off. In a gas oven, the pilot light may be enough. The trick is to try to keep the temperature constant in this range for between 3½ and 5 hours. After 5 hours, the yogurt begins to "go tart."

Don't disturb the yogurt while it is setting. When it is done, it will have the consistency of soft custard. It becomes more firm after refrigeration. The watery whey that floats to the top can be stirred back in.

VARIATIONS

Chocolate yogurt: Stir in Mom's Cocoa Syrup or 1 oz. melted semisweet chocolate after scalding the milk, or use ready-made chocolate milk, which has to be intensely chocolate flavored or the finished product will taste wimpy. Proceed with the recipe.

Caramel yogurt: Stir in the buttercream caramels after scalding the milk. Proceed with the recipe.

HOW DO YOU KNOW WHEN IT'S DONE?

There is no scientific way to tell, with clocks, or thermometers, or any other scientific tool, when something is done. It is a combination of experience and intuition.

Some people have the talent naturally. But I think a lot of people get too anxious, and don't give themselves a chance to find out if the skill is there. They want a recipe to be like a scientific training manual: do this for exactly forty-two and one-half seconds. But the real world isn't cooperative in that way. In baking bread, for instance, the interactions of yeast and flour, the humidity, and the eccentricities of the stove all play a part. And the trickster lives in the kitchen as well as in many other places.

Some things can only be learned from hands-on experience, but, as in learning to ride a bicycle, once you've got it, you can never lose it. These things include knowing when to turn a *crêpe*, knowing when an omelette is done, knowing when bread has risen enough, knowing when a griddle is hot enough, and knowing when candy has reached the proper temperature. These are not great mysteries; they are simply skills that can be learned through trial and error, although some people seem to learn faster than others do.

BLACK AND WHITE SOUFFLÉ

Serves 2 or 3

This is a recipe I devised for a chocolate cookbook, *White Chocolate*, written by Janice Wald Henderson (Contemporary Books, 1987). Even though I love soufflés, I rarely eat them and even more rarely make them myself. I wonder why? It can't be anything to do with the intricacy of the recipes, because soufflé recipes tend to be quite simple.

The black and white in this recipe are both chocolate and it is imperative that only the finest chocolate is used. White "chocolate" (it is actually cocoa butter, sugar, and stabilizers) is enjoying a trendy popularity these days, and many brands taste sweet and waxy. The only brand I like is Callebaut from Belgium.

This is something of a breakfast dessert. There's nothing here that you wouldn't eat for breakfast anyway: chocolate (as in hot chocolate), eggs, milk, sugar, and cream. It's just formulated in a different way. I'm so good at rationalization when it comes to chocolate.

I would serve this in the morning with a simple fruit salad or even a green salad or a bowl of granola. Nothing especially rich, since the souffle has enough richness for the meal. How about serving it with the Citrus Salad that appears on page 149?

2 oz. semisweet chocolate	3 egg whites
2 oz. high-quality white chocolate	½ tsp. lemon juice
3 Tbsp. milk	1 tsp. vanilla extract
¼ cup + 1 Tbsp. white sugar	Powdered sugar
2 egg yolks	1 cup heavy whipping cream

Preheat the oven to 350°.

Melt the chocolates in separate bowls over hot water. Heat the milk and the ¼ cup sugar over medium heat, stirring to dissolve the sugar. Remove from the heat and whisk in the egg yolks. Divide this mixture into two medium-sized bowls and set aside.

In the bowl of an electric mixer, beat the egg whites with the lemon juice and, after 1 minute, add the 1 Tbsp. sugar and continue beating until stiff but not dry. (The lemon juice helps to prevent dryness.)

Beat each chocolate into a bowl of the yolk, sugar, and milk mixture. You will need an electric beater to blend the white chocolate thoroughly. Fold half the egg whites into the white chocolate mixture. Using a clean spatula, fold the remaining half of the egg whites into the dark chocolate mixture.

Prepare a 6-inch-diameter soufflé mold by buttering it and sprinkling white sugar on the bottom and sides. Discard any excess sugar. Wrap a piece of cardboard in plastic wrap or foil and use it to divide the soufflé mold in half. Pour the white mixture into one side and the dark into the other. Slip the cardboard out.

Place the mold in a 350° oven for 20 minutes, taking care not to open the oven door until the time is up.

Make whipped cream by adding the vanilla and 1 Tbsp. powdered sugar to the cream and whip.

Remove the soufflé from the oven, sprinkle it with powdered sugar, top with the whipped cream, and serve immediately.

OCEAN SANCTUARY

Ocean Sanctuary is a national grassroots movement started in Mendocino, a village on a rocky headland overlooking the sea (but *not*, at least as of mid-1990, overlooking the offshore oil drilling rigs that some politicians would like to build along our coast). The goal of Ocean Sanctuary is to save the nation's seacoasts and oceans while encouraging and protecting industries such as fishing and recreation. Ocean Sanctuary legislation seeks to prohibit further oil and gas drilling, toxic dumping, and other activities which pollute and destroy.

We invite readers of this book to help in two ways: write your congressperson to urge support of Ocean Sanctuary legislation, and write for further information from the Ocean Sanctuary Coordinating Committee, P.O. Box 498, Mendocino CA 95460. (Thank you.)

BERRY-FILLED CUSTARD CRÊPES

Makes about 8 crêpes

I always keep frozen *crêpes* in my freezer so that I can assemble a dish like this on really short notice and have often done so for a spontaneous brunch. It's especially luscious with fresh raspberries or huckleberries. But I've also made it with blueberries and with strawberries and I've even tossed in a few grapes, just because they happened to be around. It's hard to imagine a fruit that wouldn't go.

"Natural" cream cheese is made without vegetable gum and as a result is fluffy and fresher. The red wine should be a decent one, but don't use that bottle of 1937 port you were given as a wedding present.

When you're making *crêpes*, be sure to understand that your first two or three are the experimental ones. You may need to adjust the batter by thinning it with a few drops of cold water. But once you've got it right and got the rhythm, you might want to go on all day. *Crêpes* will last for a few months in the freezer.

CRÊPES

6 eggs
1¾ cups milk
2 tsp. white sugar
1 cup water
½ tsp. salt

6 Tbsp. corn oil
2 cups unsifted white flour
Melted unsalted butter (for greasing the pan)

Mix all the ingredients except the butter in a blender for 30 seconds. Strain through a sieve into a container. Cover and refrigerate for at least 2 hours before using.

When ready to make *crêpes*, stir the batter. Heat an 8-inch nonstick pan over medium heat until a drop of water flicked on the surface jumps around. Grease the pan lightly with the melted butter, using a pastry brush, and pour in about 3 Tbsp. batter, tilting the pan in all directions so that the batter is evenly distributed. If there is too much, pour it back into the bowl. *Crêpes* are supposed to be very, very thin: about 1/32 inch thick.

Cook until the edge of the *crêpe* is lightly browned: about 45 seconds. Loosen with a wood or plastic spatula and use your fingers to grab the edge and flip it over. Cook for about 20 seconds more and slide out of pan onto plate. Repeat, stacking the *crêpes*.

To store, wrap tightly in plastic wrap and refrigerate for up to 3 days. To keep longer, freeze. Allow frozen *crêpes* to defrost in the refrigerator before using.

FILLING

Enough for 8 crêpes

4 oz. natural cream cheese	2 cups berries
2 Tbsp. heavy whipping cream	1/2 cup good-quality berry jam
2 egg yolks	2/3 cup red wine
2 tsp. white sugar	

Beat the cream cheese until smooth and add the whipping cream, egg yolks, and sugar. Carefully add the berries by folding them in with a rubber spatula. Try to keep the berries whole and unmashed. Ladle a generous 1/4 cup of this mixture down the center of each *crêpe* and fold the sides of the *crêpe* over the middle. Moving quickly, place it seam-side down into an ovenproof serving dish. Some of the mixture may spill out. Just replace it with a spoon.

Bring the jam and wine to a boil and stir for about 2 minutes, until slightly thickened. Pour over the *crêpes*. Bake for 10 to 15 minutes at 325° and serve.

rare or when a crêpe is done. But, with on-the-job training you, too, can become a crêpe finesser.

The first few crêpes you make will end up in the garbage or the dog, as you're trying to regulate exactly what the temperature is, and the thickness of the batter, which often needs to be thinned down a little bit with water. So you just try it and you fiddle around with it. You may waste a dollar or two's worth of batter, but finally you'll get it. I can promise you that, once you've got it, you've got it; you won't ever lose it.

At the restaurant, one person may have as many as six pans going at one time, making all these crêpes, whipping around, flipping them, and stacking them. It's a very impressive performance.

BAKED BLINTZES

Makes 6 servings

I love to serve *blintzes*, but they are a pain the neck when you have to fry them. Fried *blintzes* require a delicate touch that is not easy to pull off when several people order them at the same time and we have to keep many sauté pans going. In the interest of serving *blintzes*, I decided that we would bake them instead. Even though they don't have exactly the same effect, they are still awfully good, and probably better for you, since they weren't fried in a lot of butter.

You could place all the *blintzes* in a large pan instead of using individual baking and serving dishes, but serving them while hot can be unwieldy and unnecessarily exciting.

How does a *blintz* differ from a *crêpe*? Even in our own family, we cannot come to an agreement. My mother says *blintzes* are thinner than *crêpes*. I've always thought they were thicker. Realistically, this recipe could be described as *crêpes* with *blintz* filling.

1⅓ lb. (2½ cups) ricotta cheese
¾ lb. natural cream cheese (the type without gum)
2 egg yolks
Finely grated peel of 1 lemon
1 hefty pinch nutmeg
1 hefty pinch cinnamon
¾ tsp. vanilla extract

¼ cup white sugar
12 crêpes or blintzes (see recipe on page 176)
About 2 Tbsp. melted butter
Sour cream for garnish
Fruit: apple butter, Caramelized Applesauce (see page 25), fresh berries, or jam

Preheat the oven to 350°. Blend all the ingredients except the *blintzes*, melted butter, and garnishes together. Lay the *blintzes* on a work space in front of you and divide the filling among them, about one-third cup each, placing the filling vertically along the middle third.

Roll up and place seam-side down in individual baking dishes, 2 per serving. Brush lightly with butter and bake for about 15 minutes, until heated through. Garnish according to your wishes.

WARM BERRIES AND PEACHES WITH SHORTCAKE BISCUITS AND WHIPPED CREAM

Serves 6

A few summers ago, Beringer Winery in the Napa Valley invited a group of women chefs to prepare a lavish meal for a fund-raising event. For dessert I made this homage to delicious, ripe, fresh ingredients. You must use the best in-season fruits you can find. In other recipes, I say that it is permissible to use frozen fruits. In this one, I'm going to put my foot down and say that you really must use fresh fruit. This dessert just begs to be made fresh, because the flavors are so rich and so good.

Raspberry *eau-de-vie* is a fruit brandy, and my favorite brand is made by St. George Spirits in Alameda, California. Indeed, while the biscuits are baking, you might relax with a glass of chilled *eau-de-vie* and savor its fruit essence. (If you cannot find this particular ingredient, use a regular brandy or nothing at all if you are so inclined.)

The shortcake is very rich and light and it has just a little bit of sweetness. Short means rich, as in "shortening comma lots of." It is made with butter and cream, and there is nothing light about it.

Don't be too full when you're serving this. In fact, when serving this in the morning, I'd suggest little or nothing else with it except, perhaps, a small salad. Forget about the four basic food groups for this occasion. And forget about worrying if the shortcakes will keep. No matter how many you make, there will be none left over.

A GLASS OF WINE WITH YOUR BOILED EGG, M'SIEUR?

I love California wine and, while I know there are people who drink it in the morning, I am not among them. I'm enough of a morning person so that when I bound out of bed, I want to get on with my day.

California's wineries have been doing more and more in conjunction with food. Wine makers see how much they are interrelated with the food world and how they can make their industry much more accessible to people through food. That's why they have tasting events, distribute recipes, send out newsletters, have recipe displays in the wine sections of supermarkets, and invite people like me to develop recipes based on their wines.

FRUIT MIXTURE	SHORTCAKE BISCUITS
2 cups blueberries	2 cups all-purpose flour
2 Tbsp. white sugar	1½ Tbsp. sugar
1 Tbsp. lemon juice	1 Tbsp. baking powder
½ tsp. cornstarch	½ tsp. salt
Pinch salt	¼ cup unsalted butter, cut into ½-teaspoon-sized pieces and frozen
2 small or 1 large peach, peeled and cut into eighths	1½ cups + 1 Tbsp. heavy whipping cream
3 cups raspberries	1 egg yolk
1 Tbsp. raspberry eau-de-vie (or brandy, or kirsch, or nothing at all)	½ tsp. vanilla extract
	2 Tbsp. powdered sugar

To prepare fruit: Combine the blueberries, sugar, lemon juice, cornstarch, and salt in a nonaluminum saucepan (aluminum somehow reacts with the acid in the fruit and creates a peculiar taste). Bring to a boil and reduce the heat, simmering until a sauce forms (about 10 minutes). Stir occasionally to prevent sticking. Add the peaches and heat for about 1 minute. Add the raspberries and *eau-de-vie* and fold in carefully. The mixture should be slightly warm.

To make biscuits: Preheat the oven to 375°.

Mix together the flour, sugar, baking powder, and salt. Add the butter and blend in quickly just until the butter is broken up into small pieces about the size of peas. Add 1 cup of the cream and combine with a fork until moistened. Immediately turn out onto a lightly floured board and knead about 10 times. You want small lumps of butter to be visible.

Roll out to a thickness of ¾ inch, trying to keep the dough in a square shape. Cut into 6 squares and place onto an ungreased cookie sheet.

Mix the egg yolk with the remaining tablespoon cream. Brush on. Make a cream glaze by whipping the remaining ½ cup cream with vanilla and ½ Tbsp. of the powdered sugar. Brush this over the yolk glaze. Sprinkle with the remaining 1½ Tbsp. powdered sugar. Bake for 15 to 20 minutes, or until golden brown.

To assemble: Split 6 biscuits and place the bottom halves into 6 bowls. Add ⅙ of the berry mixture. Garnish with a dollop of whipped cream. Place the tops slightly off center and serve immediately.

APPLE BUTTER BREAD PUDDING

Serves 6 to 8

We serve this regularly in the restaurant, partly because it is so delicious and comforting, and partly because it is an effective way to use up leftover breads, croissants, and other pastries.

Neil O'Brien, who worked for us for two years, absolutely loved this pudding, but apparently he wasn't getting enough at staff meals. He noted that almost everyone preferred it warm (as I do, with whipped cream or vanilla ice cream), but he liked it cold. Somehow he regularly contrived that the bread pudding be stone cold by the time the staff sat down to eat. Until this ploy was discovered, he got all he wanted.

½ lb. cubed bread and/or pastries (we often use an assortment of odds and ends cut into ¾- to 1-inch cubes; I leave the crusts on)	2 cups warm milk (regular or low-fat)
¾ cup apple butter	½ cup white sugar
3 eggs	½ tsp. vanilla extract
2 egg yolks	½ tsp. cinnamon
	¼ tsp. nutmeg

Preheat the oven to 350°. Place the bread in the bottom of 8-inch-pan and distribute blobs of apple butter over the surface.

Beat the eggs and egg yolks together and add all the remaining ingredients. Pour the custard mixture over the bread and dunk the bread if necessary to make sure that it is soaked.

Put the pan into a larger one (9- by 13-inch is fine) and fill the outer pan with hot water, halfway up the sides. (Please do this near the stove to avoid sloshing over as you carry it.)

Bake for 35 minutes. Test for doneness with a knife. When it comes out clean, remove the pudding from the oven and let cool.

CHIPS, SURE; STALE BUNS, WELL ...

In my recipe file, I found something my sister scribbled out for me years ago, from a book we absolutely loved, called *Mrs. Coverlet's Magicians*. In the book was a recipe for bread pudding that required stale hot dog buns and chocolate chips. I remember how neat I thought that sounded back then. I keep that recipe in my file, but only as a reminder of the fact that I may have changed a bit over the years. Come to think of it, bread pudding with chocolate chips doesn't sound half bad, does it?

CREAM CHEESE AND JAM BREAD PUDDING

Serves 8

So there I was doing all these elaborate and sophisticated things, and it came to me that I wanted something simpler and more comforting. This invention was the result. It may be the quintessential comfort food. Bread puddings originated as a way to get rid of stuff that wasn't good enough for ordinary use, but they clearly hold their own as an important element of morning food. Even stone cold, straight from the refrigerator, this is very good.

In my first book, *Cafe Beaujolais* (Ten Speed Press, 1984), there was a recipe for a cream cheese and jam omelette. More than a few people told me they thought it was weird. All I can say is that one person's weird is another person's sublime. This warm and friendly bread pudding is something you either love or hate; there is no in between. To increase your chances of loving it, use the best jam you can get.

8 slices good-quality white bread, left to dry out on a rack for 4 hours (or basic home-staled bread)
1 tsp. butter
4 oz. softened cream cheese, preferably without gum

⅓ cup good-quality raspberry jam
2½ cups milk
½ tsp. vanilla extract
5 eggs, beaten
Pinch salt
½ cup white sugar

Preheat the oven to 325°.

Fit the bread into an 8-inch-square pan in two layers. Trim where needed. Remove the bread and butter the pan. Spread cream cheese, then jam evenly over the bread slices. (If this seems a little sloppy, it is.)

Put one layer of bread in the bottom of the pan, cream-cheese-and-jam-side up. Then put the second layer of bread on top of the first, also with cream-cheese-and-jam up. From the bottom, we have bread, cream cheese, jam, bread, cream cheese, and jam on the top.

Whisk together the milk, vanilla, and eggs, then strain through a sieve into another bowl. Add the salt and sugar and whisk to dissolve the sugar. Pour over the bread in the pan and push the slices down into the milk mixture to be sure they are soaked.

Put this pan into a larger one (9- by 13-inch works well) and fill the larger pan halfway with hot water. (Do this by the stove to avoid spills and sloshings.) Bake for about 50 to 55 minutes, or until a knife placed in the center comes out clean. Cool on a rack for 1 hour, then serve.

CHERRY CLAFOUTI

Serves 2 or 3

IS THE ANSWER COTTON CANDY?

The question: Is there any significant food item that is not eaten for breakfast somewhere in the world?

We don't have anything quite like this in America. You might think of it as a very French version of a very refined cobbler. I've never been a cobbler fan, but I love *clafouti*. It isn't as bready as a cobbler and it doesn't get so heavy or gluey. It is easy and simple to make and versatile enough to be a breakfast pastry or a dinner dessert. Our kitchen staff calls this "cherry clawfoot." Properly one might wish to pronounce it "cla-foo-TEE."

Clafoutis are traditional French desserts. My version has been adapted from a recipe published by Gaston LeNôtre, the famous French pâtissier. Although they are especially good with cherries, they can be prepared with various kinds of fruit, including an assortment of leftovers, if that is what you happen to have: apples, strawberries, pears, whatever. Anything but bananas or canned fruit cocktail, please. Canned fruit cocktail *clafouti* would set Franco-American relations back forty years.

1 egg	1⅓ cups pitted cherries
6 Tbsp. white sugar	3 Tbsp. melted butter (warm, not hot)
3 Tbsp. white flour	
6 Tbsp. heavy whipping cream	

Preheat the oven to 400°.

In a bowl, beat the egg and sugar with a whisk until the mixture whitens. Stir in the flour and cream. Beat until completely smooth. Pour half of the batter over the cherries in a medium-sized bowl and fold together gently.

Spread the cherry mixture evenly over the bottom of a buttered 8-inch pie pan. Bake for 15 minutes. Meanwhile, beat the butter into the remaining batter, then pour this over the half-baked cherry batter. Replace in oven and bake for another 15 minutes, or until golden brown. Remove from the oven and let cool for 10 minutes. Sprinkle with powdered sugar and serve.

STRAWBERRY-RHUBARB PIE

Serves 6 to 8

The sweetness of the strawberries and the tartness of the rhubarb balance each other so nicely in this pie.

Be sure to bake it on the lowest rack of the oven, at least for the first half of the cooking time. The reason for this is that the crumbled topping and the edge of the crust have a predisposition to burn. Heat rises, so they are further away from the heat while the filling cooks. The filling should set before the crust and topping are overdone. Use foil as necessary to protect the edges of the crust and topping from burning.

1¾ cups strawberries, quartered
¼ to ⅓ cup white sugar, depending on the sweetness of the strawberries
1¾ cups Rhubarb Glop (page 30)

3 eggs, beaten
1 prebaked pie shell (page 186)
1½ to 2 cups Crumble Topping (recipe follows)

Preheat the oven to 350°.

Toss the strawberries in the sugar. Add the Glop to the eggs and mix well. Stir in the strawberries. Pour into the pie shell. Sprinkle generously with Crumble Topping so that no filling remains visible.

Bake for 1 hour and 15 minutes, starting on the lower rack, until the center is set and the topping is golden brown.

CRUMBLE TOPPING

For this topping, the main purpose in life is to cover the filling in Strawberry-Rhubarb Pie, but it is also good on Brown Bettys and other cooked fruit dishes. "Macaroon coconut" is unsweetened shredded coconut and may be found at many health food stores.

½ cup dry bread crumbs
½ cup coarsely chopped nuts (we use hazelnuts or walnuts)
¼ cup macaroon coconut

⅓ cup brown sugar
⅓ cup flour
⅓ cup butter, cut into ½-inch cubes

Mix everything but the butter together, then blend in the butter until the mixture holds it shape when you grab a handful. Blend by hand or use a mixer. It will crumble into crumbles as you do.

CHRIS'S BUTTERSCOTCH-WALNUT PIE

Serves 9 to 10

I seem to be a pushover for things that have caramel in them, but this is probably one of the most delicious desserts I've ever eaten. Sure it is stretching it a bit to call this morning food, but it is too good to omit. Besides, some of the gooier breakfast treats such as bear claws and sticky buns come from the same family tree as this pie.

Long, long ago, my father worked as a milkman and, when he got up at four in the morning, my mother would make pie for him. So I figure, if was good enough for my dad in the early morning, it's good enough for everyone else, too. Of course I don't know if the pies my dad ate early in the morning were this goopy, or if they were healthier fruit pies. But I would have no hesitation in serving this to a milkman or anyone else in the early morning hours.

This is another one of those things that has nothing in it that's good for you. But it is so delicious and really simple to make. You can make the Butterscotch Sauce ahead of time. (And the sauce has many other uses for ice cream, hot cereal, or sneaking in big spoonfuls when no one is looking.) You could substitute other kinds of nuts for the walnuts, but I wouldn't.

2 cups Butterscotch Sauce (recipe below)
½ cup heavy whipping cream
3 eggs, lightly beaten
½ tsp. vanilla extract
1 cup walnut pieces, toasted
1 Tbsp. white flour
1 prebaked pie shell (see page 186)

Preheat the oven to 350°.

Combine the sauce, cream, eggs, and vanilla. Toss the walnuts in the flour, then distribute evenly over the bottom of the pie shell. Pour the filling over the walnuts; they will rise to the top. Bake for 40 to 50 minutes until set in the center. Allow to cool on a rack.

BUTTERSCOTCH SAUCE

½ cup butter, melted
1 cup dark brown sugar
⅔ cup light corn syrup
⅓ cup heavy whipping cream

Boil the butter, sugar, and corn syrup together gently for 8 to 10 minutes. Watch the pot carefully; it will want to boil over, but you let it know who's boss. Allow to cool for 15 minutes, then stir in the cream.

The sauce will last for quite a while if refrigerated. Should it crystallize (like honey), scoop it into a saucepan and boil gently for 2 minutes.

PIE CRUST

Makes one 9-inch crust

All too often, pies have a great potential that ends up being submerged under (and over) a soggy crust. How many gallons of delicious filling have been pushed aside by people who could not abide the limp and sodden crust? After testing countless recipes, Chris discovered one in Richard Sax's marvelous book, *Old Fashioned Desserts* (Irena Chalmers Cookbooks, Inc., 1983), a must for anyone who is serious about baking delicious desserts. I've become friends with Richard over the phone and he has kindly allowed me to include this recipe. The method of forming the shell may sound a bit complicated, but you will surely get the hang of it after one or two tries.

1 cup + 2 Tbsp. white flour	5 Tbsp. unsalted butter, cut into
¼ tsp. salt	small pieces and frozen
1 tsp. white sugar	1½ Tbsp. shortening, frozen
	1 Tbsp. ice water

Place the flour, salt, and sugar into the bowl of a food processor fitted with an S-blade and combine. Add the butter and shortening and process (turn on and off) until they are cut into the flour, about 3 seconds. Add the ice water and process for another 2 or 3 seconds, the less the better, since pie dough becomes tough when handled excessively.

Turn out onto a lightly floured board and press into a flat disc about 4 inches in diameter and 1 inch thick. Wrap in plastic wrap and refrigerate for several hours (or freeze it for use later).

Remove the dough from the refrigerator and place it on a lightly floured board. Use a rolling pin to flatten the dough, hitting down and towards the center of the circle. Move the dough in quarter turns during this step. When the dough is ½ inch thick, roll it out and continue to turn in order to insure that the surface is even. Add as little extra flour as possible and use a brush to dust flour onto the surface, if needed.

When the dough is ⅛ inch thick, lift and place it into a pie pan. Crimp the edges, trimming excess dough as necessary. Prick with a fork, then freeze for at least 30 minutes.

When ready to bake, preheat the oven to 425°. Place a large piece of foil over the surface of the dough in the pan, then place beans or rice on the foil to weigh down the dough. Keep the foil from touching the crimped edges. Bake for 10 minutes on the top shelf of the oven until the top border is set and looks more like crust than dough. Carefully remove the foil and beans and lower heat to 375°. Return the pie shell to the bottom rack in the oven and bake for 15 minutes or until the entire crust is a light golden brown. If the edges start to brown too much, cover with foil. Remove from the oven when done and let cool briefly on a rack.

CALAS

My father-in-law, Peter Kump, who runs Peter Kump's New York Cooking School, tells me that *calas* used to be served on street corners in New Orleans where deep-fried fritter-type foods are famous. I think tastes have changed over the years. I know mine have. After five or six tries, Chris and I evolved this lighter version that I really like.

Although Peter says *calas* can be served on a plate with maple syrup, I think of them more as doughnuts onto which you might sprinkle powdered sugar and cinnamon, then pick them up to eat or dunk.

You don't need any fancy or special frying equipment, just a good heavy and deep pan into which you put a few inches of peanut oil. It really helps to use a candy thermometer.

1 cup uncooked long-grain white rice	½ tsp. cinnamon (optional)
1 tsp. salt	Pinch nutmeg
6 cups boiling water	⅓ cup white sugar
⅓ cup cornstarch	⅓ cup beaten eggs (about 2 large eggs)
⅓ cup cake flour	Peanut oil for frying
2 tsp. baking powder	

Add the rice to the salted boiling water and boil, uncovered, for about 15 minutes or until tender. Drain and cool by rinsing in cold water.

Sift together the cornstarch, cake flour, baking powder, optional cinnamon, and nutmeg and set aside.

In a separate bowl, beat together the sugar and eggs until pale yellow, then stir in rice and coat well. Whisk in the flour mixture in ¼-cup increments.

In a heavy, deep pot, heat about 2½ to 3 inches of peanut oil to 375°. A candy thermometer is extremely useful here. Use a large spoon to scoop up a scant 3 Tbsp. of the mixture and carefully place it into hot oil. (Don't drop it in or the hot oil will splatter!) Fry for 20 to 30 seconds, until golden brown all over, turning as necessary. Drain on paper towels and serve immediately, either with maple syrup or sprinkled with cinnamon and sugar.

BROWN SUGAR THINS

Makes 10 dozen

These are deceptively simple (thus good to make with children) and pretty darn irresistible. I can say that authoritatively, since I ate six of them at one sitting while I was testing the recipe—all for the sake of scientific inquiry and publishing accuracy. It was important, you understand, to test them fresh from the oven, and then while they were cooling, and then when they had cooled, and when they were half an hour old, and so forth. The eating public can thank me for my devotion to duty.

I mixed the ingredients together by hand; it didn't seem necessary to get the mixer out. I softened the butter and put the whole thing together in about five minutes. You just drop little blobs onto the baking sheet. They spread out and, when they are the proper color, you take them off.

My ongoing research reveals that, on the third day, they were even more delicious, even more brown sugary and buttery, if just a little softer. They are also delicious with ice cream or sorbet.

2 cups unsalted butter, softened	Pinch salt
2 cups light brown sugar, firmly packed	½ tsp. cinnamon
	1 tsp. vanilla extract
2½ cups white flour	2 large eggs

Cream together the butter and sugar, mix in the flour, salt, cinnamon, and vanilla, and add the eggs, one at a time, beating after each one. Chill for at least an hour.

Drop 12 scant teaspoons onto an ungreased cookie sheet and bake at 350° for 9 to 10 minutes, until the edges are brown.

Cool for 30 seconds before removing from pan. Use a metal spatula and lift each cookie off the pan carefully and place it on a cooling rack. Let cool thoroughly, then transfer to an airtight container.

These cookies last for a week at room temperature and much longer when frozen.

Despite the occasional complaint letter, I love to open mail. That's a job I don't think I would ever delegate to someone else. If you write to Betty Crocker or Aunt Jemima, she probably won't open the envelope herself. Write to me, and you can be sure that I will. I try my best to answer all letters that request replies—but I am not perfect. I am regularly impressed by how heartfelt the letters are, and how articulate the writers are. How could I fail to respond when they have taken time out of their busy lives to write to me, a complete stranger—and yet they seem to feel we are already friends.

When my pen pals visit the restaurant, it *is* like meeting a friend. But it's also rather odd, since I know almost nothing about them and they know so much about me: Someone I have never seen before is asking me about Mom and Dad, and my sister back East, and life in Mendocino.

GINGER SHORTBREAD

Makes 12 pieces

This is a recipe I devised for *Food and Wine* magazine for an article on Christmas cookies. There are never too many kinds of shortbread and, since I like ginger and I wasn't aware of a ginger shortbread, it seemed a logical thing to try.

It is impossible to mess up this recipe, so it's another good one to make with children. The mixture is just "smooshed" in the pan and then baked. You don't even remove it to cool it. I use candied ginger, which I find in the Oriental food section of the supermarket. It usually comes in round coin-shaped pieces, but thicker than a coin.

Traditionally, shortbread is not supposed to brown, but I prefer a slight toastiness. Let your own preference rule. Traditionally, also, shortbread is marked with the tines of a fork, either for decoration, or to facilitate cutting or breaking it into pieces, or perhaps for some mystical Scottish reason.

2 oz. candied ginger
⅔ cup unsalted butter, at room temperature
½ cup powdered sugar (sifted *then* measured)

⅔ cup all-purpose flour (sifted *then* measured)
¾ cup cornstarch (sifted *then* measured)

Preheat the oven to 325°.

Slice the ginger into little sticks or batons about ¾-inch long, like short fat toothpicks. Butter a round 9-inch cake pan with unsalted butter.

Depending on how much you like to have a hands-on (or -in) experience, you can mix the ingredients together with said hands, a wooden spoon, or an electric beater. In any event, cream the butter until it is quite soft. Add the sugar, flour, and cornstarch and blend thoroughly. Mix in the ginger, distributing it evenly.

Turn this mixture into the prepared cake pan, using a rubber spatula to scrape off fingers or beaters. Press the dough as evenly as possible into the pan; it will be sticky.

Holding a fork vertically, divide the circle into 12 pie-shaped sections. Then use the tines to press a pattern of lines around the circumference of the circle, about half an inch long.

Bake for 30 to 35 minutes, shifting the pan if necessary to prevent uneven baking. Remove the pan from the oven and use a knife to re-mark the holes because they will have partially baked together. Cool on a rack.

FRUIT AND NUT CARAMEL SHORTBREAD

Makes 16 to 20 rich pieces

This is really a goopy mess that some people will say doesn't belong at the breakfast table. But children will love it and enjoy helping to make it. Adults are hardly likely to turn their backs and walk away from the table. After sampling it more than a few times, it came to me that this is the perfect recipe for people who like to get up in the middle of the night and nibble on forbidden foods. It is very sweet.

The recipe comes from Barbara Holzrichter, whose caramel factory has been described in other places. If you are unable to use her wonderful product (see page xv for ordering), store-bought caramels will do.

1 box (18 oz.) Grand Finale buttercream caramels or other caramels	1 cup chopped pecans
	¾ cup butter
1 Tbsp. half-and-half	¼ cup white sugar
1 cup chopped dried apricots	2 cups white flour

Preheat the oven to 350°.

In the top of a double boiler over low heat, melt the caramels. Remove them from the heat and blend in the half-and-half, apricots, and pecans. Set aside.

Beat the butter with sugar until light and mix in the flour with a fork or your fingers. Press this dough into a greased 7- by 11-inch pan. Bake for 15 minutes, then remove pan from oven and pour the caramel mixture over the top. Return to the oven and bake for another 10 minutes. Cool, then cut into bars.

ALMOND-FILLED BUTTER CAKE

Serves 12 to 16

This is an authentic Dutch recipe from Jocelyn Kamstra, who cooks at the restaurant and bakes in our brick oven. I'm always tinkering with other people's recipes, whether from books or friends, but this one is just right as is.

The word *cake* is something of a misnomer, since this one is anything but light and fluffy. In fact, it is rich and dense, in the European manner, and best served in thin slices. For people who don't require a large and well-balanced breakfast, a slice of this and a cup of coffee might well get them through to lunch.

Crusts with a lot of butter don't do well in the refrigerator; the butter tends to congeal. Happily, this cake will last a week or more unrefrigerated, and the odds are very high that there won't be any left by then.

CRUST	FILLING
2⅔ cups white flour	1 cup finely chopped almonds
1⅓ cups white sugar	½ cup white sugar
1⅓ cups cold, unsalted butter	2½ tsp. finely grated lemon peel
½ tsp. salt	1 egg, slightly beaten
1 egg	12 whole almonds, for garnish

Preheat oven to 325°. Grease a 9- or 10-inch springform pan. Combine all the crust ingredients in a mixing bowl. Using an electric mixer or a food processor fitted with a steel S-blade, blend until dough forms. Chill for about 10 minutes. Divide the dough in half. Spread one half on the bottom of the prepared pan and keep the other half refrigerated.

In a small bowl, combine all the filling ingredients except the whole almonds. Spread the filling over the dough in the pan to within ½ inch of the edge. Between two pieces of waxed paper, press or roll the remaining dough into a 9- or 10-inch circle. Remove the top layer of waxed paper and turn the dough over the filling. Remove the remaining waxed paper and press the dough into place. Garnish with 12 whole almonds in a pleasing pattern.

Bake in the center of the oven for 50 to 55 minutes, or until a light golden brown. Be careful not to underbake. Place a cookie sheet on the lower rack to catch any spillage. Cool for 15 minutes, remove sides from the pan, and cool completely on a rack. Do not refrigerate but do keep tightly covered. Keeps for 1 week.

people who have perhaps given up their customary oat bran muffins just for this one meal.

That's the way I think of this book. Put your meals together anyway you wish, but don't write me angry letters about how I am ruining people's lives with all this rich food. Anyway, to some extent, I *have* moved in a healthier direction. In most recipes, I have found that yogurt works as well as sour cream, sometimes better, and so that's what I'm using now.

In high school, I always used to drink nonfat milk with my chocolate brownies. Somehow I felt that they cancelled each other out. We each make peace with our scale in our own way.

MUTTI'S MARBLE CAKE

Serves 10 to 12

For many years, I have been carrying a scrap of paper in my recipe file. On it are the ingredients for a cake listed in a fading European script, but no instructions. This "recipe," from Elsa Kent, was given to me by her daughter, Laura Katz, who said, "You're the great cook; you figure it out."

I have been a little daunted by this challenge. At a certain point in the recipe testing for this book, I felt overwhelmed and turned to my husband for help. He valiantly took my crumpled piece of paper and a few hours later emerged from the kitchen with a delicious marble cake. This elegant and refined cake is made all the more special with the chocolate glaze.

1 cup unsalted butter, softened	¼ cup unsweetened cocoa powder
1¼ cups white sugar	2 Tbsp. milk
4 eggs	3 Tbsp. sugar
Grated rind of 1 lemon	2¼ cups white flour
¼ cup rum	1 Tbsp. baking powder
1 tsp. vanilla extract	½ cup warm milk
¼ tsp. salt	

Preheat the oven to 350°. Beat together the butter and sugar until light and fluffy. Add the eggs one by one, then the lemon rind, rum, vanilla, and salt. Don't worry if the mixture looks curdled; adding flour will fix it.

Warm the cocoa, milk, and the 3 Tbsp. sugar together to dissolve the sugar and make a dark cocoa syrup. Sift the flour and baking powder together and add in three batches to the egg, sugar, and butter mixture alternating with the ½ cup warm milk, beating between each addition. When the batter is smooth, divide it in half and mix the cocoa syrup into one half.

Fill a buttered and floured 9-inch loaf pan with alternate layers of the two batters: white, chocolate, white, chocolate, white. Use a knife to swirl the two batters together. Do it with a light touch and do not blend them.

Bake for 60 to 70 minutes until the cake tests done. Cool on rack for 5 minutes, then unmold. Serve as is, or drizzled with Chocolate Rum Glaze.

CHOCOLATE RUM GLAZE

Makes ¾ cup

3 oz. semisweet chocolate	1 Tbsp. instant coffee (dry)
3 Tbsp. rum	3 Tbsp. butter, softened
3 Tbsp. water	

Melt together the chocolate, rum, water and coffee in a double boiler over low heat. Whisk in the butter until smooth. Let this cook for about 10 minutes until slightly thick and drizzle over the cake.

MOM'S ALMOST-UNBEARABLY-DELICIOUS CHOCOLATE FUDGE

Makes 1 serving for those who regard a 9- x 9-inch slab as a serving

This sweet has almost nothing in it that is good for you: no oat bran, no yogurt. That being the case, it has an obligation to taste as good as it possibly can.

If you do not already eat fudge in the morning, you are hereby granted permission to do so. Think of it as a very delicious cup of superb hot chocolate that has somehow cooled and congealed. If you're not ready to eat it straight, you might want to crumble it into either hot or cold cereal.

The recipe comes from my mom's highly esteemed collection. It was written in her unique style: illegible and unintelligible. Fortunately she was at my side, interpreting as we went along. The faded index card stated: "Beat till thickens." So I'm beating and beating and beating and finally I ask her how long I am supposed to do this. She says, "Oh, for a very long time; it could be fifteen minutes or more. Everybody knows that." And when it finally did begin to thicken, she cried, "Be careful! It can turn grainy at any second." This hair-raising experience yielded a most delicious fudge. I think my directions are sufficiently clear so that we won't have to include the 1-800-CALL MOM help number in the book after all. And it really *was* worth it, because this is truly an almost unbearably delicious fudge.

The necessity to beat fifteen minutes with a wooden spoon may seem onerous, but I strongly recommend your doing it by hand, at least the first time, so that you can clearly observe the physical changes: The sheen disappears quickly, and the fudge grabs the spoon.

Neither grainy nor sugary, it is dark and rich and smooth. I intentionally don't specify the kind of nut, because any kind will do, and each one from the traditional walnuts or almonds to hazelnuts and Brazil nuts to indulgent macadamias, gives the fudge a somewhat different personality. In the unlikely event that any is left over, it can be frozen.

3 cups white sugar	1¼ cups butter
1 Tbsp. gelatin	2 tsp. vanilla extract
1 cup milk	1 cup chopped toasted nuts
½ cup light corn syrup	(any kind)
3 oz. bitter (unsweetened) chocolate	

Mix together the sugar and gelatin in a large pan. Add the milk, corn syrup, chocolate, and butter. Cook to soft-ball stage (236°, or see the no-thermometer way to tell, at right).

CHEMISTRY IN ACTION

In many recipes, precision is not essential. A minute or two more or less; an oven setting twenty-five degrees either way won't make much of a difference. But candy making is pure chemistry and it really calls for precision. You can either use a candy thermometer, or use the following method to determine when you are at "soft ball" stage: At the point at which you think it might be ready, take a tiny bit of the hot liquid fudge and drop it off the spoon into a bowl of cold water. With your fingers in the water, try to make a soft ball out of the chocolate glop. If you can, then you have achieved "soft ball" stage (which is also one of the markings on a candy thermometer).

Pour into a large bowl. Cool for 15 minutes, add the vanilla, then beat like crazy with a wooden spoon until the fudge thickens. It could take 15 minutes. The glossy appearance on the surface will dull, and the fudge will thicken suddenly and "grab" the spoon. When this happens, quickly add the nuts while stirring and pour into a lightly buttered 9-inch-square pan. If you dawdle at this stage the fudge may turn grainy.

Cool, cut, and insert a piece in your mouth as quickly as you can.

DRINKS

CREAMY APRICOT DESSERT FLOAT

Serves 3

A few years ago, I was asked by the Canned Apricot Advisory Board to come up with a recipe. I honestly couldn't think of anything too wonderful to do with canned apricots, in heavy syrup no less, and then the idea of a drink came into my mind. Then I converted it to dried apricots, even though the Dried Apricot Advisory Board has yet to call. It tastes great either way. Everything is put into the blender or food processor and spiced up a bit. The drink is served with ice cream and a cinnamon stick.

If I were serving this in the morning, I'd at least consider offering it just as a drink, without the ice cream, but where is it written that you can't have ice cream for breakfast?

This recipe is impossible to wreck. You can use more or less syrup or apple juice, depending on how thick you want it. The alcohol is optional, but it does a good job of accentuating the flavor of the fruit. If you use dried apricots, there is no added sugar in it so the mixture is rather tart.

6 oz. dried apricots or 1 can (17 oz.) apricots in heavy syrup	Pinch cloves
	3 Tbsp. dark rum or brandy or apricot brandy (optional)
2¾ or ¾ cups apple juice (for dried and canned apricots, respectively)	¼ tsp. vanilla extract
	1½ cups vanilla or apricot ice cream (optional)
¼ tsp. ground nutmeg	3 cinnamon sticks
¼ tsp. cinnamon	

Place the apricots and about half the apple juice in a small pot and bring to a boil. Cover and simmer until very soft and mushy, about 30 minutes. Stir occasionally. Pour into a blender or food processor and purée.

Add nutmeg, cinnamon, cloves, rum or brandy, vanilla extract, and the remaining apple juice. Stir to blend and heat gently. When the mixture reaches a boil, remove from heat and pour into three heatproof glasses or mugs. Add ice cream and garnish with a cinnamon stick.

WITH SPOONS ON THEIR NOSES AND BELLS ON THEIR TOES . . .

I came back from San Francisco one day, and all the people on the staff had spoons hanging from their noses. I said, "I've only been gone a few days; how have you learned how to do this wild thing?" They provided lessons. You take the spoon and, making sure there's no grease on your nose, try to hang it there. After maybe five or six times . . . suddenly a spoon is hanging from your nose. So we all raced outside for the photo: front and side views. Do you suppose Wolfgang Puck or Alice Waters can hang spoons from *their* noses? Are there any old tintypes of Escoffier with a spoon hanging from his nose? Perhaps a wooden spoon?

Sometime soon after, in the middle of dinner service, some of the customers saw a member of the staff doing it in the back. Suddenly these dressed up people, the customers, amid the formality of white tablecloths and all, had spoons hanging from *their* noses. It's apparently quite contagious.

KEMPER'S DRINKS

While the rest of the world may think the restaurant business is glamorous, we in the kitchen know it to be stressful, exacting, and hot. Often during a particularly frantic period known to some as "lunch," someone will ask, "Are we having a good time yet?" At that moment, a cool drink is the closest thing any of us will have to a good time until the craziness is over.

Michael Kemper, an artist who worked for us for a while, invented these two refreshing drinks. The nonalcoholic Domestic Wet is a mixture of flavors that include tart and sweet combined with a bubbly fizz. The Wet and Wild uses the same flavors together with wine and champagne, so we save it for the end of the shift. Here at the restaurant we use the Pinot Noir grape juice and the Gewürztraminer produced by Navarro Vineyards, a local winery in the Anderson Valley. But any grape juice will do, as will almost any white wine that is not piercingly dry. We serve the drinks (to ourselves and to the customers) with a brightly colored straw and a fuchsia or other color-coordinated, preferably edible flower or a sprig of fresh mint.

DOMESTIC WET

Serves 4

1⅔ cups grape juice
¾ cup freshly squeezed grapefruit juice (try to get a ruby grapefruit for a colorful touch)

1¼ cups soda water

Mix together quickly and pour into glasses over ice.

WET AND WILD

Serves 4

1⅔ cups grape juice
½ cup freshly squeezed grapefruit juice (ruby preferred)

¾ cup Gewürztraminer or other white wine
1½ cups champagne (an inexpensive one will do fine)

Mix together quickly and pour into glasses over ice.

LEMONADE

Makes about 8 servings

What is there to say about a simple, perfect lemonade, except to remind people that it is "just" another citrus drink, as suitable in the morning as are orange or grapefruit? This lemonade is intended to go over a lot of ice, because it is very concentrated. The purpose of the simple syrup is to allow you to have the sugar in a drink entirely dissolved. It is a useful thing to know for almost any drink. This lemonade is also good for adding to iced tea.

I prefer to use fresh lemon juice. I think it's a great deal better than the kind you buy in bottles or small plastic replicas. At the restaurant, we use a fair amount of lemon peel, so we end up with numerous naked lemons. Sometimes we use cases of lemons in a relatively short time, so we freeze quantities of lemon juice.

¾ cup Simple Syrup (recipe below)

1¾ cups freshly squeezed lemon juice
3½ cups warm water

Mix all the ingredients together and serve over ice. Garnish with mint.

SIMPLE SYRUP

½ cup warm water

1 cup sugar

Place the water in a small pot. Stir in the sugar until it is dissolved. Bring to a boil and let cook uncovered for 5 minutes without stirring. Remove from heat and let cool, then refrigerate if not needed at once.

brake on, leaped out, and begun screaming bloody murder. I became the kind of hysterical woman I had thought only appears in comic books and situation comedies. If there had been a chair, I would have been on it, clutching my skirt, if I had been wearing one.

Can you imagine the prospect of driving along a winding road with a car full of slithering live eels on the loose? This particular renegade eel happened to slide over my brand new Marimekko bag, sliming it for life. The fact that it was only one of a crateful of eels didn't make me any the more rational. By now, I was completely out of control, screaming, "Kill it, kill it!" Chris calmly said, "No, we can't kill it. We paid good money for it." I assured him that I would buy it out of my personal allowance. He countered with the scenario of some poor unsuspecting sheep farmer coming upon a dead eel and wondering how many sheep this evil thing had killed before it met its own end. Eels do bite, you know.

Finally Chris found a big stick by the side of road. He was able to stun the eel just for a moment and lift it back into the crate. We drove very carefully on to Mendocino.

But wait, there's more. The next evening

RHUBARB SYRUP

As we made various rhubarb dishes and drinks, we found we had a by-product: this Rhubarb Syrup, which became the prime ingredient in both the Rhubarb-Lemonade Fizz and the Rhuby Cocktail.

Rhubarb syrup left over from making Rhubarb Glop (page 30)	Lemon juice

Bring syrup to the boil. Skim the foam that rises to the top and reduce by one-third. Add lemon juice to taste. Don't overcook or the syrup will turn caramelized and brown.

RHUBARB-LEMONADE FIZZ

Serves 1

It's refreshing, cooling, and delightfully different. We serve this often on hot summer days. Well, we don't have that many hot summer days, so we serve it on mild summer days, and cold winter days, and whenever else we feel like it.

1 Tbsp. Rhubarb Syrup (see recipe above)	Soda water to taste
⅓ cup Lemonade (see page 199)	Ice
	Sprig mint

Combine the syrup, lemonade, and soda water. Add ice cubes and garnish with mint.

RHUBY COCKTAIL

Serves 1

One of the great things you can do with Rhubarb Syrup (see recipe above) is to add a tablespoon to a fair to middling champagne and make a nice aperitif. The acid of the rhubarb cuts the inevitable sweetness of most less-than-expensive champagnes.

1 Tbsp. Rhubarb Syrup	1 glass champagne

Stir the one into the other.

---

the dinner staff came in, prepared to cook weekend food until the wee hours of the morning. All the eels had escaped this time, squiggling and wiggling out of the crate onto the floor. It was like something out of the Bible. Wasn't there something about a plague of eels upon your house? Even if there is no mention of them there, these are creatures disgustingly appropriate for plagues.

And the end of the story is that it turned out to be extremely difficult to prepare and cook the eels. We ended up spending about fifteen hours to do something that those more knowledgeable could have done far faster. If only we had known. Somehow I never enjoyed the terrine that we finally made and I am *not* including any eel dishes in this book. If you have some eels to cook, you're on your own. Don't call me, and I won't call you.

They ask if this business is a hard one. Let me tell you: To my dying day, I will never forget that sight in the rearview mirror of the top of the crate askew and the last few inches of eel slithering off.

HOT CHOCOLATE

Serves 4

We serve a great deal of hot chocolate in the restaurant, both with and without Mocha Whipped Cream (recipe follows). Sometimes I think people would be astonished if they realized the quantities one must make of certain things, even in quite a small restaurant like mine. We make five gallons of this recipe at a time, and it lasts us two or two and a half days.

If you have a steamer (the kind found on an espresso machine), you can use it to make a frothier drink, which I find wonderfully comforting.

    4 cups milk
    3 Tbsp. white sugar

    6 Tbsp. sweetened hot
        chocolate powder
    3 Tbsp. unsweetened cocoa

Place all the ingredients in a saucepan and whisk over medium heat until combined. Serve hot or cold.

MOCHA WHIPPED CREAM

Makes about 2 cups

This little recipe has no redeeming social values whatsoever, other than the fact that it tastes so good. I use it to make double hot chocolate in the restaurant or to garnish coffee drinks.

You can use it with almost any kind of pastry dish, from *crêpes* to *calas*, and it isn't half bad if you just happen to get some on your fingers and have to lick them.

    1 cup heavy whipping cream
    4 oz. semisweet chocolate,
        chopped

    4 tsp. instant coffee
    1 Tbsp. white sugar
    2 tsp. vanilla extract

In a small pot over low heat, warm all the ingredients until the chocolate is melted. Then whisk to combine. Pour into a bowl, cover, and refrigerate until very cold (at least 4 hours). Whip before serving.

NAMING RECIPES

I am not tied to any of the names of my recipes. Sometimes I name them just because I have to call them something to be filed alphabetically, either in my computer or in my box of recipes. "Toasting Bread" (page 55) is right up there in the cleverness sweepstakes with "Bowl of Cereal."

Once I named a soup Mama Nini's Soup. (Nini is one of our three dogs, 2.5 Labradors, and all gourmets.) I made this soup in honor of her on the day she had a litter of puppies. People loved it and, for all they knew, Mama Nini was someone's wonderful Italian neighbor who had created the soup back in Italy eighty years ago; obviously the real thing. My mind was very full of Nini and her endeavors. It seemed right to honor her at that moment with this soup, which you will find in my *next* book.

When I was five, my
mother made a chocolate
sauce that I remember as
being extraordinarily delicious. She used it to
make chocolate milk. I
thought this would be a
perfect recipe for this
book, whether for milk or
hot chocolate. So Mom
made it just the way she
did when I was five, and I
was not wildly enthusias-
tic. Prompted by the
sophistication I have
probably acquired since I
was five, I said, "Well,
maybe you should put
some coffee in it, too, to
enhance the chocolate
flavor."

What is happening,
then, is that some child-
hood "favorites" really
need to be revamped to
fit in with my ideas and
tastes today. So the rec-
ipe is not authentic
1950s Mom, but the feel-
ing is authentic.

MOM'S COCOA SYRUP WITH A DIFFERENCE

Makes about 3¼ cups

The memory of a delicious chocolate milk from my childhood inspired this recipe, an adaptation of my mother's from about thirty years ago. She and I fiddled and fiddled with the ingredients until we had a product that met the expectations of our taste buds.

The cinnamon and to some extent the coffee give it a Mexican flavor. But my mother became nervous about that. Being a fiend for authenticity, she decided she would be more comfortable if it were called Mom's Cocoa Syrup *with a Difference.*

Despite the presence of both chocolate and coffee, this drink doesn't taste at all like mocha.

1 cup cocoa	3 oz. grated semisweet
1½ cups white sugar	chocolate
Pinch salt	2 tsp. vanilla extract
1 cup hot water	¼ tsp. ground cinnamon
	1 tsp. instant coffee granules

Mix together the cocoa, sugar, and salt in a saucepan and slowly stir in the water. Continuing to stir constantly, bring to a boil and boil gently for 3 minutes. Remove from heat and add the grated chocolate. Stir, set aside and, when cool, add the remaining ingredients. Refrigerate.

To make hot or cold chocolate: Stir together 1 heaping Tbsp. of the syrup and 1 cup milk. I especially like this drink steamed and dusted with cinnamon. If any is left over, store it in the refrigerator.

Index

in coffee cake, 69
in muffins, 44
and prune filling for coffee
cake, 71
in shortbread, 190
in waffle sundae, 88
Peppers. *See* Bell peppers
Pesto, 139
in cheese *strata*, 155
for pizza, 161
on polenta, 167
in sandwich, 117
Peter Kump's New York
Cooking School, 187
Pie
Chris's Butterscotch-Walnut,
185
Strawberry-Rhubarb, 184
Pie crust, 186
Pineapple, chunky sauce of, for
waffles, 89
Pine nuts
in omelette filling, 98, 100
in pasta sauce, 136
in *pesto*, 139
Pizza, Judy's "Instant," 161
Plums, poached, 28
Polenta, Creamy, 167
Poppy seeds
in filling, for bread, 60
in muffins, 43
in salad, 148
Potato
in *alpbacher gröstl*, 162
fried, 168-169
pancakes, Oma Leah's, 81
red, omelette of, 106
salad, Pam Michels's
famous, 150
Priano, Patricia (Tricia), *69-70*,
163
Prudhomme, Paul, *89*
Prunes
and pecan filling for coffee
cake, 71
in tea, *28*

Pudding, Tex-Mex Cornbread,
156-157
Pumpkin
canned
discussed, 82
and ginger, in pancakes, 82
soup of, 125
fresh, muffins of, 43

R

Raisins
in bread, 54, 58, 63
in cookies, 35
in muffins, 45
in rolls, 53
Raspberries, and peaches, with
shortcake, 179
Relish, *Pico de Gallo*, 141
Reynolds, Robert, 87
Rhubarb
Glop, 30
in pie, 184
in sandwich, 120
and strawberry pie, 184
syrup, 200
Rice
in *calas*, 187
China Moon Shanghai, 159
wild, in waffles, 85
Rolls, Cinnamon, 53

S

Salad
Chris's Waldorf, 147
Citrus, 149
Egg, 118
Margaret's Walking, 147
Pam Michels's Famous
Potato, 150
Pasta, 151
Salmon, sandwich of smoked,
119
Salsa, 140
in *Huevos Rancheros*, 109
on *polenta*, 167
Salt, kosher, discussed, *140*,
159n
Salzburger Nockerl, 113

Sandwich
Creamy Mozzarella, 117
Egg Salad, 118
Open-Faced Smoked Salmon,
119
Smoked Turkey Salad, 120
Sap, maple, 21
Sauce
Butterscotch, for pie, 185
Chunky Pineapple, for
waffles, 89
Cranberry, 130
Goat Cheese Pasta, 136
Smoked Turkey, for waffles,
135
Spicy Sausage, for pasta, 137
Tomato-Eggplant, 138
in Catalan Omelette Cake,
196
on polenta, 167
white, 111
Sausage
andouille, sauce of, 137
in baked apples, 31
in hash, 163
linguisa, sauce of, 137
in omelette, 98
as *polenta* topping, 167
sauce of spicy, 137
Sax, Richard, 186
Schwartz, Naomi, 90
Shortbread
Fruit and Nut Caramel, 190
Ginger, 189
Sobel-Feldman, Susan [pseud.
F.L. Florian], 44
"Soft-ball," described, *193*
Soufflé
Black and White, 174-175
Ole, 112
Spinach, 111
Soup
Grandma Kump's Lo-cal
Asparagus, Tarragon, and
Garlic, 124
Pumpkin and Tomato, 125
Spinach and Mint, 126